TIANGELLO T. HILL

Before You Do

HOV Publishing a division of HOV, LLC.
www.hovpub.com
hopeofvision@gmail.com

Cover Design: HOV Design Solutions
Editor: Amy A. Owens for Clarity Communication
Proofreader: Dianna Knox-Cooper

Write the Author Tiangello T. Hill at traej22@yahoo.com

For more information about special discounts for bulk purchases, please visit www.hovpub.com

ISBN 978-1-942871-60-6
Library of Congress Control Number: 2019937434

10 9 8 7 6 5 4 3 2 1

Printed in the United States of America

DEDICATION

To My Mystery Woman

Somewhere between almost and not yet, sometimes I think you're soon to come, but other times it appears that you'll never arrive. However, I think that you should know that I'm a better man and a wiser man because of all that I've experienced before meeting you. While I'll never make you any empty promises that I cannot fulfill, I can assure you of a few things. I can assure you that you'd never have to worry about anything or anyone else having my attention. I can assure you that you'd be adored and loved without restraint and unconditionally. To be honest, loving you and the different ways to love you are all I think of even though I don't even know who or where you are. I'm always thinking of how much more creative I can be along with the different ways to make you feel me mentally, physically, emotionally, and spiritually. You'd be my central focus. You'd be the goal I'd seek to accomplish and the mission I'd try to fulfill. You'd be the world in which I live and the reason for my being. I seek to lose myself in you. So much so that I no longer think of me but everything is you and you alone. The fulfillment of your satisfaction and your praises are what I seek to fulfill and accomplish. The true essence of my being longs for your arrival, your touch, your kiss, and to live life with you. This life and this world are so cold and lonely without you. Please get here soon! I have so much to give you, so much to show you, so much to offer, and so many ways to satisfy you and to love you!

Patiently waiting...

Before You Do

TABLE OF CONTENTS

OPEN LETTER TO LOVE

Dear Love,

There are some things I've wanted to say to you. While I appreciate how you've made me feel, you've afforded me a few moments that I'll always cherish and never forget. The lessons you've given will forever remain with me. However, there are a few problems that I have with you. Now, before I say what's on my mind, please understand that I'm not angry, nor am I bitter. There are just a few things I need to get off of my chest. First of all, I don't like the company that you keep. Your influences have caused me to fall for a few people who either didn't mean me well and had no good intentions concerning me or who were manipulative enough to make me feel right while they were killing me softly. Secondly, viewing people through your lens has caused me at times to be more committed to them than they ever were to me and to give multiple chances to those who didn't deserve chances at all. Your perspective caused me to fall and even feel for those without restraint whose intentions weren't genuine or authentic. Because of the kind of person that I am, along with your influences, I have with no limit loved in spite of who can't seem to love me enough in return. Finally, one lesson you should have taught me, that I had to learn on my own is, while there's nothing wrong with loving hard or even loving fast, you shouldn't love everybody from a romantic perspective. I've learned that some people are just good to admire from afar, some people are only good to know as an acquaintance, and others need to be left where they are. In spite of it all, I love how you make me feel;

I love seeing how others respond to the creative things you influence me to do when I'm involved with them, and I can't wait to give my all to that one individual who reciprocates it in return. I have these issues with you that have forced me to control you until the day comes when I can trust you enough to flow freely through me with someone who appreciates having me.

CHAPTER 1

Loving the Wrong One the Right Way

Moment of truth: Many of our frustrations, fears, and phobias about relationships have derived from the fact that we've spent too much time loving, dating, and investing our time in the wrong people. We've been giving the best and better parts of ourselves to people who didn't deserve our time and attention, nor did they deserve to enjoy the privilege of our company. However, because we were either tired of being alone, we were willing to give the benefit of the doubt, or because we were finally ready to take a risk, we have given chances to people whom we should have allowed to keep it moving! Now that it's all said and done, we realize that they were just a waste of our time, energy, and attention. As a result of these deadly encounters, many people make the mistake of judging everyone in their future based upon everyone in their past.

Consequently, we can conclude that the real issue of distrust isn't with the people you are yet to meet; it is with the people you've already encountered. However, what happens is that you end up taking out all of your frustrations on the people you are yet to meet penalizing them for behavior that someone in the past exhibited in your life. Not only is this unfair to the person/people you will encounter in your future, but it is also unfair to you as well. You cannot blame someone or hold someone at fault for who you choose chose to love last year. The person in your present didn't tell you to love them, they didn't ask you to give them a chance, nor did they obligate you to remain committed to them when they did you wrong.

You chose to date that person, forgive that person, and give that person another chance when you already knew what they did; and you wanted to HOPE that they would love you right and treat you right when they had already shown you that they didn't have your best interest at heart.

As a result, there must be some degree of confrontation that you have with yourself and within yourself. This confrontation must not only cause you to realize that you chose to love the wrong person(s) in the right way, but it should also provoke you to forgive yourself for doing so and not view everyone else from the same perspective because of what may or may not have happened in your past relationship experiences. The more significant issue is allowing yourself to heal and then possessing the ability to free yourself from the imprisonment of the pain caused by the people in your past.

When you live the rest of your life punishing others for every offense people have committed against you in your life, it is a clear indication that you haven't given yourself the opportunity to heal from the past experiences. You may say that you have because you've moved on to a new relationship or new lover when the truth of the matter is you haven't. Had you allowed yourself to heal you wouldn't be holding your new mate in suspicion for every little thing that they do. The times and moments when you say that your current mate has done something to remind you of what your last mate did are not an indication that your new mate has done something out of order necessarily; it's proof that you have allowed neither your mind nor your heart to heal.

"Stop being a convenience
for other people's indecisiveness!"

It is also legitimate proof that you haven't freed yourself from the imprisonment of the pain the people in your past have caused you. You say that it's hard; I say that you don't want to free yourself and that you're living a guarded life. You say that people do you wrong when you let them get close to you or make yourself vulnerable to them; I say that there's a difference between allowing someone in, versus letting someone take advantage. I say that there is a difference between falling for someone and falling in love with someone and being someone's fool. Love doesn't make you ignorant! Love doesn't make you blind! Love doesn't make you naive! Love doesn't make you foolish! Love doesn't make you weak! Instead of becoming bitter and angry at everyone else in your future, you should become wiser and be cautious.

You cannot live the rest of your life guarded, restricted, or bitter especially if you're one who desires and enjoys relationships and companionship of any kind. You rob yourself, your heart, and your emotions of the physical contact that we were created to have and experience. For even a more straightforward rebuttal, if you gave yourself to all of the wrong people, you should very much so give yourself to the right person. Well, at this point you may very well be asking what you did wrong to be in such a position. The answer and diagnosis of that are simple. You could have spent more time listening than watching. Anyone can tell you what you want to hear, and the issue is whether or not they can perform what they bragged about. Just like our criminal justice system states that defendants are considered innocent until proven guilty. The reality is that defendants are treated as if they are guilty until proven innocent.

With that being said, remember the old saying; Actions speak louder than words? When someone 's actions contradicted what they were saying, you should have been following your head, rather than your heart, seeing that they weren't honoring what was promised to you, or what they said to you. Secondly, you could have very well rushed things or allowed them to push you quicker than you were ready to advance. No matter how you feel, what you feel, or the intensity of your feelings you still have to take your time. Rushing will always cause you not to see what's really there and it will also cause you to miss what you need to address and be aware of. While you may make yourself vulnerable to them, you must also maintain some degree of control. Why rush if we have the possibility of spending the rest of our lives together? We have a lifetime, and it's a marathon, not a sprint race! Meaning, it's best to pace ourselves because we have a ways to go; there is no need to rush to see who's the fastest to finish.

Finally, you allowed your love or your feelings to make you recklessly offer too much trust too soon. Again, I continue to say to you that love doesn't make you ignorant! Love doesn't make you blind! Love doesn't make you naive! Love doesn't make you foolish! Love doesn't make you weak! You are still a living being who must be responsible because at the end of the day people can only do to you what you allow or permit. So, while you are trying to crucify them, also remember that there's a certain degree of responsibility you have to bare as well. Here's the twist, though you must be responsible, you also must understand that there is a difference between insecure and guarded versus being sure and cautious. There is a thin line with this issue as well because not being sure and careful enough will make you naive and reckless. Being too confident and overly cautious will make you insecure and guarded.

However, my intent in this chapter is not to damage you more than your previous relationships have already damaged you. My intention is to help you heal from loving the wrong people the right way to help you love the right person in every right way. Let's talk! There are four things in particular that you need to embrace to receive your proper healing regarding this situation.

LOVE DID WHAT IT WAS SUPPOSED TO DO

One thing you cannot do is fault love for love. Love is consistent; love makes you feel the way you need to feel and the way you want to feel. Love gives you the reason for what you do and who you are to whomever you're in a relationship with. In other words, love ALWAYS does what love is supposed to do; love always does its job. You don't have a problem with love because love has never done anything to you except what it was supposed to do. However, your problem is with the person(s) you chose to love. Love has never hurt you! Love has never lied to you! Love has never betrayed you! Love has never cheated on you! Love has never physically, verbally, or emotionally abused you! Love has never taken advantage of you! Love has never taken your kindness for weakness! Love has never played games with you! Love has been completely true to you! It's the people from your past that have done these despicable things to you.

Therefore, instead of talking about never being in love again or how badly love hurt you, you must learn from past experiences and make better decisions regarding who you choose to love from here on out. Let's be brutally honest for a moment because you've been hurt and disappointed, and you're responding and making a judgment of future relationships based upon the negative experiences that occurred in your past relationships. As a result, you have compiled all of the negative experiences together to form analysis and conclusions about everyone else you may encounter in the future. When in fact, there was once something good about these supposedly bad past relationships that initially provoked you to invest your emotions and love.

There was a season during these previous relationships when something about them caused you to develop feelings and fall in love with them prior to them hurting you. That love made you stay with them, believe in them, take a chance on them, and risk everything for them. Why? Because that's what love is and that's what love does. Love has done its job while the person you chose to love betrayed your trust or broke your heart. Love is not at fault; SOMEONE is at fault.

Thus, you cannot possess ill feelings towards love or about love. Understanding your pain and hurt, you can only hold accountable the entity which caused all of these negative emotions. Love cannot offend, nor does love abuse; it just brings you to a level of emotion causing you to make particular sacrifices for the person who is the recipient of your love. Therefore, running from love is unnecessary and unfair to you. No matter how guarded or insecure you may be, you can't control love. It happens and evolves even when you don't plan on it or anticipate it. Once it's provoked, you can try to deny that it exists, however, when it's real and authentic you know that its present.

"Don't focus on being so independent that you fail and forget how to deal with authentic companionship and assistance when it comes."

YOU'RE NOT THE BLAME

The fact that you truly loved them caused you to do what you did for them and make the sacrifices that you made for them. With this in mind, you did what ANYONE who is genuinely in love with someone should have done. You cared for them, you catered to them, you supported them, you sacrificed for them, you were there for them, you may have even claimed their children as your own. You were faithful to them, you were committed to them, and you also believed in their potential and dreams when they didn't or could see it themselves. You weren't stupid for doing so. You weren't even their fool for doing all that you did for them. However, you did what a person in love was supposed to do; it was your responsibility as their mate to do for them all that you did because of your love for them.

The dangerous thing about love, loving, or being in love is that when you choose to love someone who you're not supposed to love or be with someone you know you can't have. Or when you choose to love someone who is supposed to be off limits to you because one or both of you is either married or involved with someone else YOU ARE THE BLAME. As much as people deny it, it's suicide when you put yourself in a position where you've allowed yourself to fall in love with two different people at the same time. Therefore, you must always be in constant communication with yourself regarding whether or not the love you are developing is healthy. Just because you can and are allowed to, doesn't mean that you should. Especially when the person you're trying to love or the situation itself is not a favorable situation for you and your well-being.

However, when the setting is genuine, and the proposition or person is legit, though the relationship itself may not work or last, you cannot blame yourself for the love that you had or the things that love made you do for that person. You did what you were supposed to do and what you should have done. It's not your fault or love's fault; the person you loved didn't appreciate you or your feelings for them. Which ultimately gave you a reason to do all that you did for them while you all were together and involved. Love, when it's authentic, can't be manipulated or controlled. Therefore, we must at all times use extreme caution when it comes to allowing people to awaken the love that we have to offer.

As will be discussed in another chapter, Givers must always be aware of those who are Takers. For when the Giver operates with no restraints, it is relatively easy to be taken advantage of by those who are Takers and don't appreciate what a Givers brings into their life. Consequently, because you give your all when you love, you must learn to be particular when releasing yourself to people who you engage. There's nothing wrong with being this kind of person. And still, everyone doesn't deserve to have someone like you because they don't know how to embrace someone with your magnitude of liberty and love.

BE CHOOSEY IN YOUR NEXT CHOICE

Just because you've been propositioned or you see someone who meets your taste or attraction doesn't mean that you have to accept or pursue them. While it may feed your ego and self-esteem to have someone show interest in you, or perhaps you've seen someone that may be attractive to you, their proposition or that particular person isn't always what you need for where you're going or what you're doing. The fact of the matter is, everyone doesn't deserve to be in your life relationally! Therefore, you must be extremely selective when it comes to choosing, and being chosen as, a mate. Though the invitation may be there and though the opportunity may have availed itself, you have to look past the attractiveness of the person and the proposition to discern whether or not this person will fit with who you are and where you're going.

Often, people have accepted propositions or pursued others based on situational disappointment and relational depravity. In other words, many people have just accepted anything and anyone due to the mere fact that they're tired of being alone. Or, it may be just because out of all the dead-end relationships they've had in the past, this person said the right things or acted the right way, and they were under the assumption that they may have found the right one. While this may seem complicated, it's very simple and easy to understand. If you wouldn't go to the mall on a Saturday and start giving random people your birthdate and social security number, why would you accept any random person's proposition or pursue some random person just because of their looks or something that they said? Selectivity is very critical when it comes to who you will be involved with. EVERYONE is not compatible with your spirit, EVERYONE is not compatible with where you are in life right now, and EVERYONE is not compatible with your life's destiny. Therefore, you must learn to not only be choosey but be very selective as well.

"Who's really at fault, the one who did it or the one who allowed them to do it because they didn't address certain issues when they occurred?"

Now don't be mistaken, physical attraction is necessary and essential. Even having the ability to communicate effectively is of extreme importance. However, when you get beyond what you see and the words spoken, you need to investigate whether the individual you have pursued or who has pursued you, is indeed compatible. Prayer alone won't work at this point! You will have to interact to properly investigate while learning how to break away and cut it off at the appropriate time if that person is not for you. Thus, with this in mind, some people ruin good possibilities because they're either being overly spiritual with no natural balance, or they are entirely too carnal with no spiritual involvement and foundation. YOU MUST HAVE BALANCE IN YOUR LIFE!

Just because something is offered doesn't mean you have to accept it. Just because something is made available doesn't mean you go after it. So, it is with the people you encounter! However, this part of the involvement is not just all about who propositions you or who you may come across that appeases your eyes. Yet, there is a part you play in this as well knowing what you want, knowing what you need, knowing where you're going, and knowing what you're trying to have. Without knowing these things you'll accept anything and anyone to claim that you have a mate, only to spend months, perhaps years, with someone to eventually realize that they aren't what you want and you aren't what they want. They may have had certain benefits; they may have even possessed specific attributes, but THEY weren't what you wanted or needed. The key component here is knowing or at least have an idea because your life and future are far too important for you to be trying to figure out along the way what is it that you want or what is good for you. It's a waste of their time and yours, and more importantly, it's unfair to them. Cease from doing trial runs with your life and your relationships.

TAKE YOUR TIME

Why be in a hurry for somebody who you realized, in the end, should have been irrelevant to you? If they are rushing you in the acquaintance process, be concerned. Investigate, slow down, and pay attention because you shouldn't be in a hurry to go anywhere and to have nothing. Don't be afraid to let them go if they are threatening to leave you, claim that you are slowing them down, or if they are in a hurry for what you're not ready for. For if you're serious about dating in the pursuit of marriage, you cannot make decisions inspired by impulse, desperation, or even loneliness. Take your time; this is your life, and it is your entire future that's at stake. Why, if it's real and if they are truly yours, you will have a lifetime to do and accomplish everything that you desire.

While time may be of the essence, in this case, time is certainly on your side. Take the time to get to know them. Take the time to find out why they are the way that they are and why they do what they do. Take the time to discover what's in their heart and what they are made of. Take the take to find out the type of spirit that they have. Take the time to see how they compliment your life. Take the time to see if you like their other side, the side that's the everyday them (the side no one would like if they saw it). TAKE YOUR TIME...It's a marathon race, not a sprint race. In this case, what you don't know really can hurt you. Not only do you need to know but you also need to see it. Far too often, people commit themselves, their emotions, and their heart to people without even really knowing who they are committing too. Neither your heart, your emotions, nor your life can afford to take another relational disappointment. Therefore, it would behoove you to take your time and see everything for what it is and for what it is not.

No one is worth another heartbreak! You should also have had enough of picking up the broken pieces of a battered heart that occurred as a result of giving yourself to the wrong person. So, use time to your advantage and find out about the person you've propositioned and vice versa. If you lose that person, or if it doesn't work out, always remember that they are not the only human being who has been created. Do yourself a favor and take your time; it's not worth the rush.

OPEN LOVE LETTER

Dear Mystery Woman,

I envisioned you coming home to me, how we greeted each other when you arrived, and how the rest of our evening went. We embraced and held each other tight. We shared a passionate kiss, and you told me how much you missed me while I told you how much I loved you. We sat for a while and talked, all the while knowing what we couldn't resist. Trying to be cordial, trying to be intellectually influenced, and trying to appreciate the presence of the company of the one the both of us have been longing for. However, being honest with ourselves there was no denying what the moment was. You couldn't resist me; I was craving you, our hands took a mind of their own — no need to set the atmosphere because the mood has been established from the very onset. The fire was lit, the right music was playing in the background, and there was an attraction between us that you called chemistry, but this is what we've dreamt of. Reflections and shadows of two people intensely intertwined appear on the walls from lights shining so dimly, in a room that's not just filled with two bodies, but with an intense passion and ecstasy that demands and warrants the secretions of something undeniable. Words were said, but it didn't matter what they were. It sounded so seductive, sexual, and sensual that whatever it was I'm sure it was right. You took hold of my arms and proceeded to grab and gravitate to the center of my back, caressing, clawing and even squeezing as the pressure built and the tension increased. I heard your voice ever so passionately. You told me you loved me, and I told you how much I needed you. You convincingly whispered how you wanted me. I said let's make a family. I gently tipped your face to look into your eyes. Then, as always, you disappeared in my sleep while still proving that you are the woman of my dreams.

Signed,

The Man of Your Dreams

CHAPTER 2

Side A and Side B

There is an initial phase of getting to know someone. For the first three months you conversate, spend time together, do activities together, and go places together. You begin to build what you think is a rapport with that person and a solid foundation. You start to relax and allow your guard to come down, ultimately falling for that person and what you believe is a genuine and authentic relationship. Your feelings begin to evolve and get stronger. Shortly after that, you bring them around your family, and if children are involved, you introduce them to your children under the impression that what you have with this person is real and secure. Eight months to a year into what you once believed was a secure relationship, and something happens between the two of you where you are left to say to them, "You've changed," or "I thought you were someone different when we first met." You are embarrassed and even humiliated that you got involved with such a person because you brought this person around your family and children. Ultimately, you find yourself alone all over again.

However, on the flip side, you may have met someone who presented themselves in a certain light and what or who they presented themselves to be wasn't necessarily real. You fell for who you thought they were, or rather who you wanted them to be, without even scratching the surface to know who they truly were. To aid in your falling for them, they continued to feed you with who they wanted you to think they were. However, when they finally realized that they had you all tied up and connected to them, they switched and showed you the side of themselves (their Side B) that you had never met, the real them. Leaving you confused and even dumbfounded, after you come to your senses, you realize that you fell for a person that didn't exist. You begin to understand that the person you thought you knew was only an illusion; a sales pitch to get you to a place to deal with or entertain a person who you would normally never give attention too.

Finally, you've met a person of whom you felt was attractive and possibly a good candidate for a life-long relationship. You like what you see, you like what you hear, and you even like what you feel. However, even though the beginning is good because everything is new and fresh, you begin to wait them out to see what else there is about this particular person that you need to know and see. Eventually, you start to notice certain things, that are possible deal breakers, that concern you and that lead to other covered issues that you need to be aware of. While the person may not necessarily be a bad individual, you've been able to see all aspects of them (the good, the bad, the ugly). In other words, you've had a chance to see their Side A and their Side B. Side A was their first-impression self; that side of them that got your attention and piqued your interest. Side B, however, is that side of them that either convinces you that you need to move on and run like hell, or it shows you what you will have to deal with if you remain involved with that person.

"Stop cluttering important space with the presence of unnecessary people!"

SIDE A AND SIDE B

The issue with a person's Side A and Side B is centered around false advertisement. However, it can also be a matter of misinterpretation on your behalf. Let me explain! A person who approaches you or someone that you may be interested in can present to you one person, the illusion in which they want you to buy into. While at the same time being a completely different person who possesses a different personality with different habits. Someone who approaches you, or someone who you may be interested in, may not show everything up front to make sure that you're present in their life for the right reasons. However, because you do not see what you want to see, or you do not hear what you desire to hear, you decide to walk away thinking that this is a person that's not compatible with you. Now we have an issue of misinterpretation on your part because you decided against them based on the presentation of their Side A when their Side B could have been what you were looking for.

Dealing with this situation almost makes you feel like you're stuck between a rock and a hard place, which is the main reason why, as mentioned in the previous chapter you have to take your time and do your research while also knowing when to cut it off if need be. Consequently, it forces another topic of conversation to be held which forces us to address how much you present when initially meeting someone, and at what point you should leave some things untold and unseen. My conclusion to that is simple; show and express enough to gain their interest and to keep them coming back for more. However, don't show and reveal so much that you make yourself appear cheap or desperate, or to put yourself in a position where they are only coming to you for one thing. You have to decide what's enough and what's not enough. If you're going to entertain someone for a possible relationship, you can't be so guarded that you aren't willing to share certain things about yourself or you aren't allowing them to get close to you. Otherwise, please stay by yourself, leave them alone, and don't waste their time or yours. There's nothing more frustrating than trying to be with someone or be involved with someone who has so many walls built up that you can’t get to know them; you can't ask them certain questions, nor are you given a real chance to love them or get to know them. Why? Because their walls go up the moment, you get close, and the moment that both of you begin to develop feelings they either run away or push you away.

Simply put, when presenting Side A, you must do so with restraint, discipline, discernment, and wisdom. By now you've been through relationally enough and have had enough disappointments that you should know what you're up against and what to look for during the actual engagement. Consequently, there are some things about their Side B that we need to address to help you better understand when it’s time to walk away versus when it’s time to roll up your sleeves and work on building a relationship because no one is perfect. The perfect person doesn't exist. You aren't perfect. So you can end your search for the perfect partner. Not only is there no such thing as a perfect person, but there is also no such thing as a perfect relationship. However, it’s how two persons choose to deal with the problems in their relationship that makes their relationship perfect.

THE SWITCH UP

There are some individuals that you may meet who presented themselves as a person who you were extremely attracted too. However, by the time you see their Side B, you realize that you’ve met a completely different person who you are unattracted too. They’ve done what I call The Switch Up. They influenced you to buy into a portrayal or an illusion of themselves that wasn't real at all, and you were under the impression that you were getting one person, while you were getting a person who you never even desired to know. You are left to wonder how you allowed yourself to get involved with such a person. In all truth, IT WASN'T YOUR FAULT!

The fact of the matter is, once you embraced the initial attraction of the person you were involved with, they presented you with an illusion of what and who they wanted you to buy in too. They conducted themselves in a certain way, they conversed with you in a certain way, they behaved in a certain way, and they treated you in a certain way. Consequently, you invested yourself into something and someone you assumed to be genuine and authentic. You developed love and even began to fall in love with this particular person. Everything about you, what you thought, and how you felt regarding this specific person was contingent upon what and who they portrayed themselves to be to you. However, the issue is the person you grew to know and grew to love never existed. You developed expectations and even aspirations for a person who not only never existed but who also wasn't real.

The conflict with this situation lies in the fact that you have begun to establish a life and hope for a future with a person you were presented, all the while being involved with a complete stranger and someone who you don't know. You become completely invested and they expose who they really are only after you've made yourself completely vulnerable, giving them access to your personal and private life, and have brought them around your loved ones and friends. You indeed experienced THE SWITCH UP! In other words, this person exposed you to someone that you never knew nor expected. We cannot even say or suggest that they changed because

"Stop wasting people's time
who never asked you for your attention!"

they were always who they eventually showed you they were. Their real self was suppressed beneath the representative that they presented to you. Their true ways, their true perspective, their true attitude, along with their true identity were hidden by their *Side A*. Their *Side B* was a completely different person! The Switch Up can be very hurtful because it's usually covered in deceit, lies, and manipulation to say the least. It is the reason why many people in this day and culture almost run away from relationships and people all together. The Switch Up is what causes people to have their guard up at all times and not trust anyone. However, while we know everyone makes life changes periodically, please understand that making changes over time has nothing to do with people performing the Switch Up or portraying themselves in certain ways when they're someone and something else.

The reason the Switch Up is so dangerous is that those who do it are usually those who come into the relationship with the intention of advertising one thing but offering another. They can't be trusted, and you never get the chance to feel comfortable with them out of fear of another Switch Up. During the Switch Up is when you find out that they possibly have a family that you didn't know of or that they have other secrets you didn't know of. These people may also live lies; they may not have the things they told you they have, they aren't doing the things they told you they were doing, nor are they headed in the direction in which they suggested. The issue with those who are practitioners of the Switch Up is that in many cases it's hard to tell them apart from those who are authentic and genuine. It is so critical that we learn to ask questions, acknowledge red flags when they appear, and be willing to respectfully call people out on things that are just not right. In many instances, we've seen certain things, and when we look back in retrospect regarding those who have switched up, if we had ignored the red flags, we would have been able to save ourselves much heartache, disappointment, and time. Therefore, it is critical that we not be in a rush or overly excited when it comes to presentation and give those who approach us or those who we entertain the time to reveal their *Side B*. In doing so, you provide them with the opportunity to show whether or not their Side B is a Switch Up or is it their *Authentic Self*; Let's go deeper.

THEIR AUTHENTIC SELF

Regarding people's Side B, when a person is transparent enough to show you their Side B up front, it is no longer considered a Switch Up; this person is showing you Their Authentic Self. Therefore, it becomes your responsibility to decide to stay and deal with it or leave and find someone else. They didn't hide anything from you; they were completely transparent about who they were and who they weren't. In the words of southerners, "They put it all on the table!" They allowed you to see their flaws and their struggles, along with their good. They told you where they've failed, where they struggle, and what it is they intend to do. They have allowed you to see how they think and what they like or don't like. Therefore, they gave you the opportunity to decide to either leave or remain in the relationship. These persons did not rob you of your right to choose! Now, here's the important component about people showing you Their Authentic Self; THERE IS NO PERFECT PERSON! There will be something about every person you meet that will require you to decide whether or not you can live with them and Their Authentic Self, or if it's too much for you to deal with. So, for those of you who continuously go from one person to another and from one relationship to another while claiming each previous person had too many issues that you couldn't deal with, keep in mind that there is something wrong with all of us and each of us has things that others don't like about us. To be honest, it may be that it is yourself that you are running from!

Some people's problem when it comes to dealing with the Authentic Self of others is that often when people are exposed to the Authentic Self of their potential mate, there is a proclivity to try and change their Authentic Self so that it is to your liking. You may try to change the way that they think, the way that they talk, the way that they act, or something else about Their Authentic Self so that it better suits you, but not them. Your efforts to change something about Their Authentic Self reveals your level of contradiction and confusion. On the one hand, you claim that you want someone to be truthful and upfront with you, yet on the other hand, when you finally meet someone who gives you transparency your immediate response is to try and make them change Their Authentic Self. While you and your mate should motivate each other to do better and to grow, it is unfair to your potential mate for you to try to impose on them your ideas of how they should be just because they may have something about them that you don't like. Again, when an individual allows you to see Their Authentic Self, it is your decision to choose whether or not you're going to leave or stay. Look at you, you either just met them or you're in the beginning phases of getting to know them, and you're already trying to change them or get them to change only to accommodate you. All the while, they are letting their guard down for you to see who they really are. How inconsiderate, self-centered, and self-aggrandizing you are!

"You can't expect positive results when you constantly create a chaotic environment."

It is not their fault that they showed you who they are; it's your fault that you stayed with someone whose ways you were not able to handle. As a result, instead of either being honest enough to either walk away, mature enough to evaluate your own ways to see if you actually could be compatible, or just accept them for who they are, and are not. Your comfort technique and security reaction caused you to immediately try and get them to change instead of accepting them for who they are. However, in accepting them for who they are, you also are choosing to stay with them and accept them for who they ARE NOT. It is no one's job to change to make you comfortable or happy. Honestly, you wouldn't want anyone doing that to you. You can accept a person for who they are, and who they aren't, or you can't. For a person to change who they are to appease you means that sooner or later they will be unhappy with themselves, and unhappy with you. The two of you will likely still end up parting ways anyway. For someone to expose to you, Their Authentic Self is a clear indication that they feel comfortable enough with you to see them in their absolute purest form.

When accepting someone's Authentic Self, you put them in a position where they don't have to put up a facade or portray themselves as someone who they are not. You allow them to feel so comfortable that they expose information of importance that may very well be critical to how you should handle them or what their intent is for being in your life. You must have a disposition and presence that will encourage someone to expose Their Authentic Self to you. Consequently, another issue is raised that needs to be addressed. Did the person pull a Switch Up on you and hide their Side B, or did you portray yourself a different way to the point where the other person didn't feel comfortable exposing Their Authentic Self to you? All the blame cannot be put on others for not exposing Their Authentic Self to you; you have to ask yourself what role you played in them not feeling comfortable enough to do so. It is your responsibility as their mate, or potential mate, to make them feel comfortable telling you everything about themselves and their situations. All the while, knowing that if they are transparent, you won't use what they expose about themselves against them. Nor would you use what they revealed to you to judge them. Far too often our mates don't disclose things to use because they either feel as though they can't talk to us about anything out of fear of either being judged, criticized, humiliated, or embarrassed by the person they should feel free to talk too.

When a person to shows you their Authentic Self, it is proof that you have created for them an environment wherein they feel comfortable being transparent with you. This kind of person is to be respected and applauded. However, many people fail to appreciate this magnitude of authenticity and transparency because in today's culture and society we look for reasons to leave and run from relationships instead of searching for reasons to stay in relationships. When you come across someone who trusts you with this part of themselves, if you can deal with Their Authentic Self, you may have very well come across someone special enough to hold on to and fight for. After all, it's one thing for a person to disrobe and be nude in your presence. However, it's when a person disrobes their true identity to you, that your relationship reaches another level. Are you mature enough to be entrusted with caring for someone else's true self? Or are you still operating in a spirit of selfishness, demanding that others accept you for who you are without you accepting them for who they are?

DECISIONS

Once you've seen a person's Side A and Side B and you realize that they have not performed the Switch Up on you, but they have exposed Their Authentic Self to you, you have a few decisions to make. Will you leave or will you stay? If you're going to stay, are you willing to accept them for who they are and for who they're not? If you decide to stay, you must realize the information they shared with you cannot be utilized for any other reason or purpose other than learning how to love them. You have to understand that if you chose to use the information about their Authentic Self against them, there is a strong possibility that they will never share anything of transparency or importance with you again. There is a thin line between someone feeling the need to make themselves vulnerable with you and feeling the need to shield their truth from you. If you chose to stay with them in spite of their Side A and Side B, you must handle their Authentic Self with extreme care.

Should you choose to leave because of their Authentic Self, you must leave knowing that EVERYONE has an Authentic Self that you may not be able to or willing to handle. Therefore, since everyone has an Authentic Self, it would behoove you to adjust your perspective of how you deal with people or the type of people you can deal with. For this reason, many people are single and may forever remain so because they refuse to adjust themselves to deal with this particular component of maintaining relationships with other people. As one old man told me, “When it comes to choosing a woman, all of ‘em are crazy!” You have to choose what level of crazy you're willing to deal with and go with it! I'm sure women say the same thing about us. With this being said, stop looking for the perfect person because the perfect person does not exist! Though you're looking for your soulmate, please understand that your soulmate is going to come with an Authentic Self that you're going to have to choose to deal with or leave alone. We all have to work with each other in spite of our Authentic Self to make the relationship work and succeed.

Consequently, you have some decisions to make since you're so tired of being single and alone. You have some decisions to make since you're ready to live your best life and share goals with someone you love and who loves you. You have to decide to stay and accept them or leave and continue your search for the perfect person that doesn't exist. You have to decide to love them in spite of or to reject them because of. Either way, you have to make a decision. That's not their responsibility but your responsibility. To simplify it even more, making this decision has everything to do with you deciding to be with someone or deciding to remain single. Make a decision!!!!!!

...in a world where loyalty is not valued, trust is often betrayed, promises are broken, words have no meaning, sacrifice is unappreciated, exploits are soon forgotten, oaths have no substance, touches are made with no passion, "I love you" is randomly used, everything seems to be temporary, relationships are one-sided, we post one thing but live another, people want "real" when they're fake, demands don't meet expectations, and compromise is replaced with selfishness.

CHAPTER 3

Changing The Rules of The Game

We can unanimously agree that before the development of feelings, the discussion of a possible future, or interactions of any kind, there must be some rules or guidelines established before anything evolves between the two of you. Guidelines and rules are necessary for any relationship to be both successful and effective! They establish expectation, confidence, as well as, consequences. In other words, guidelines are necessary because not only do they allow you to have an idea of what to look for and expect, they also inform you of the method of operation of the relationship along with what are deal breakers with the person in which you are involved with. When guidelines have been put in place, the other party that you're involved with cannot say that they didn't know you weren't interested in this, or you didn't want to participate in that. Why? Because the guidelines and rules had already been established.

Having guidelines and rules should be implemented as a sense of structure and discipline and not for the sake of one controlling the other. The guidelines must be mutually agreed upon and not implemented selfishly. These guidelines should not be from the spirit of dictatorship or one ruling the other with an iron fist. However, these guidelines should be for the sole purpose of showing the other how to love you and to make sure that the relationship is functioning in such a way that both parties are in agreement with. Guidelines must be specified, unanimous, and collectively created in the beginning, not made up as you go. You must NEVER recklessly engage in a relationship with anyone establishing rules or guidelines as you go. That is a guaranteed way to experience a disaster. GUIDELINES MUST BE MADE AND IMPLEMENTED IN THE BEGINNING! It is not a matter of imposing self-will; however, it's making sure we see what we desire.

The issues with guidelines come when they have been agreed upon and implemented, and one desires to change them for selfish reasons or to keep from being responsible concerning an issue in the relationship. In other words, there is an attempt to alter guidelines when one doesn't want to face the consequences for their actions, or they don't want to take responsibility for an offense or wrong that they've done. These guidelines should be used to help develop the foundation of the relationship and that by which the two should govern themselves in the relationship in order to complement each other. They should not be abused, negated, or abandoned! Any relationship that doesn't have any guidelines is a relationship that's doomed and destined for disaster. These guidelines should encompass the rules of the relationship itself, the rules of compatibility and attraction, the rules of appetency, and the rules of restriction and freedoms all of which we will discuss in depth in this chapter.

"Don't ask for my attention when you have no intention of maintaining my attention."

THE RULES OF THE RELATIONSHIP

Prior to developing serious emotional ties and feelings along with a serious commitment, general rules for the relationship need to be established. Rules that address how you will function as a couple, how you expect to be treated and respected, along with how you like to feel and what you need to see being their mate. These rules will enable you to establish a firm foundation for your relationship and will also allow you to establish an absolute magnitude of trust in the other person. In all truth and actuality, you should investigate and ask questions regarding their concept of relational rules to assist you in deciding whether or not to engage with them in a relationship of any kind. For example, you should discover what their beliefs are regarding building a family, establishing your own family traditions, as well as, their beliefs involving the inclusion and exclusion of others in your relationship.

It is critical to establish these rules up front so that there is a clear understanding of what's going to transpire and how things will flow once the relationship has begun. Where there are no rules, there is no discipline, and where there is no discipline in a relationship, there will always be recklessness and carelessness, which leads to disaster in the highest degree. These rules are important because when you know what they expect, you get an idea of who you're dealing with and what it will require to be involved with them. So, in the process of asking what turns them on, what they are attracted too, and what pleases them you must also learn to ask what their rules are. Initially, they may give you silence and may even be somewhat shocked at the question and ask themselves. Why? Because most people live and jump in and out of relationships only having an idea of what they want or what they're looking for. Based on the bad experiences of their past, they can also clearly tell you what they don't want. However, very few people have specified what their relational rules are and can barely put it into words when asked. As a matter of fact, unless they are a quick thinker and are extremely intellectual, you may get the response that says they never thought about it or no one has ever asked them that particular question before.

The fact of the matter is, you not only need to know their rules but you also should know your own. Don't complain about the company that's at your table when you don't even know why you're at the table or what you bring to the table yourself. Knowing your rules and knowing the rules of others will help you remove what you don't want and who you don’t want in your life from a relational standpoint. Everyone won’t be able to meet or live up to your rules, nor will you be able to meet or live up to other's rules. Why? Because everyone's not meant for you, nor are you meant for everybody. So, knowing your rules and knowing their rules are very critical and essential for the success of any relationship. It’s important to know because you don't need to be with anyone who doesn't believe in disciplining their kids while not only do you believe in disciplining your kids but your kids are made to leave the room and the house when grown folk are talking.

Who ever knew loneliness could be so lethal? the absence of the one you absolutely desire causing so much distress...Who ever knew that this kind of love could evolved so quick? Yet some say that they don't believe in love at first sight...Who ever knew that this kind of connection would go far beyond compatibility? Some people never find this in a lifetime, being so innocent yet so true...Who ever knew that missing someone in such a way would leave you longing just to hear their voice? There are those who can go a whole day with no interaction or communication at all, however, seemingly totally unbothered. Who ever knew that something so new could have every indication of being so everlasting? However, what's lasted long doesn't always have to be good.... who knew? Who knew? Who could have ever known?

Consequently, it’s important to know the relational rules for both parties involved. So, while you're asking where they work, where they live when was the last time they were in a relationship, what happened to cause their last break up, also ask them to be specific in telling you their rules. Once you discover what their rules are you may realize that they may be handsome or attractive and made exactly the way you like, but their rules may be a deal breaker for you. Know your rules and find out what their rules are!!!! It’s the life or death of your possible relationship! Their rules can be the hindrance or the success of your relationship. Don't be afraid to ask questions, however, don't be afraid to specifically say what you like or don't like or what you do and don't expect.

THE RULES OF COMPATIBILITY AND ATTRACTION

What attracts you to me? What makes us connect? What has us "feeling" each other? What has me wanting to see more of you? What has us staying on the phone all night? What has us even willing to take a chance and risk our meeting each other to pursue a relationship? Why are these questions essential for this particular rule? Many people know how to get into a relationship, they know how to engage in certain activities that the relationship provides, and they know how to engage with a sweet person. However, the issue for a multitude of people is how to get into a relationship without knowing how to make one work or last. Thus, many people jump in and out of relationships, and they go from one bed to another or from one marriage to another because they don't know how to make a relationship work. Anyone can get into a relationship but it takes a consistent and responsible person/people to make a relationship work.

Far too many people love the look of a relationship, the feel of a relationship, and even the benefits of a relationship but can't do the work of being in a relationship. What good does it do for the two of you to be compatible and attracted to each other without necessarily knowing how to stay together. So, the real question should be, "I like you and may even love you, but can I live with you? Yes, we work well together but are we still good together now that the newness of the relationship is gone?" When we find the answer to these questions, we then can find the real reason of why we are together and the direction the potential relationship is headed. When all of these questions are answered, it also helps you understand what separates your mate from the rest and why you even made them your choice in the first place. The reason why this is essential is that you will eventually come across someone who's more attractive than your mate or someone who may even have more to offer. However, because your mate is your choice and these questions have been answered, you may see that the grass looks greener on the other side, but it's best to stay in the grass that you helped plant and nurtured to grow.

The rules of compatibility and attraction encompass a number of things such as finding out what your mate is attracted to, what makes them attracted to you, and why are they interested in you. It involves you also doing whatever is necessary to maintain that attraction and interest once you find out what it is and why. The rules of compatibility and attraction demand that you find creative ways to continue to feed what drew them to you in the first place. Far too often we get involved with people only to change everything that drew them to you and the things that made you all compatible in the first place. However, you change or rid yourself of what initially compelled them to be involved with you, yet you so quickly become insecure when you notice them giving observance to what it is they like. Attraction and compatibility go hand in hand because they open the door to conversations of intellectual dialogue that exposes personal insecurities, interests, and expectations that causes the other party to evaluate their real intent and purpose for being present.

OPEN LOVE LETTER

Hey Sweetie,

I begin by saying that I love you and because of who you've become in my life along with the person you are to me, I'm falling in love with you more every day. Every time I hear your voice, I fall more in love with you. Every moment that we share together, I fall more in love with you. However, I'm perplexed right now. I hate hearing tension in your voice. I hate seeing you frustrated. I don't like seeing you go through. I can't stand to see you or hear you dealing with your struggles knowing there's nothing I can do to rectify your problems. My intent and reason for being in your life is not to complicate or confuse your life. However, my intent and reason for being in your life is to simplify and to bring peace to your life and situation. Your hurt, your frustrations, and anything that brings contention in your life is my weakness. They disturb my peace. It aches my soul in the most aggravating way imaginable.

I know issues will arise and problems will occur; however, when you're not smiling or filled with the ebullience that comes as a result of being with me. I can't handle it because in this world I've been created for you, for us. What you're stressed about, frustrated with, and continuously upset over doesn't exist with me or when we're together. I want to rescue you from your struggles, alleviate what you're currently concerned about, and dissolve what's hindering your advancement. The very thought of you crying over this or shedding tears over that without me being

able to wipe your tears and to offer you the consolation that you deserve won't allow me to rest. Where are you? When will you come? Why aren't you here? How long will it be before you take your rightful place by me? How much longer shall I long for you? You're healing is here with me, your satisfaction is here with me, and your future is here with me. I have a love for you that far exceeds your previous experiences and expectations. I love you Mystery Woman! Where are you? I won't stop until I find you, until I have you here and until you're living life with me...
Loving You,

Your Future

CHAPTER 4

Close All Exits

I am almost certain those who remember when can unanimously agree that when it comes to relationships and dating everything has changed compared to the way things used to be. Even the music we listen to has drastically changed. In this day and age, it seems that hardly anyone wants to be truly and fully committed. People would rather say, "We're just talking," "We're cool," or "I just have friends." All of which are ways of saying, "I have people that I do things with, but I'm not committed to anyone." It appears that everyone wants to enjoy the company or the benefits of having a certain kind of company without really committing to that one person. In doing so, this gives them the liberty to go out and do what they want, when they want, with whom they want without being accountable to the person whose company they frequently enjoy.

Regarding the music, there was a time when everything we listened to pertained to love songs. The groups and various singers we admired sung about how to make love work, how to make love last, and how to come back or reunite with the one you love. Even if the one you loved was the one you lost or the one who left, even if you were the reason for them leaving.

In today's society, the music we listen to reflects what is going on in relationships. The songs focus on cheating, having multiple partners, secret lovers, and indulging in multiple affairs. Hardly anyone is singing about being committed to ONE PERSON, loving ONE PERSON, or making it work with ONE PERSON. There was a time when the groups and various songs we admired sung about how to make love work, how to make love last, and how to come back or reunite with the one you love.

In conjunction with the music, other media outlets are doing the same. We see more on television about cheating spouses and secret affairs than we do about THE FAMILY sticking together and making things work TOGETHER. Thus, this society has developed and grown people who have a like-minded mentality. Hardly anyone wants to be committed, and there are so many who wants to enjoy the benefit of multiplicity instead of being satisfied with singularity. Consequently, the conclusion of the matter is simple. Today's culture spends more time feeding their own greed and self-centeredness, to the point to where family, as we grew up to know it, is slowly fading into the abyss.

Though it doesn't seem like it, there are still people looking for that one person to whom they can be fully and totally committed, build a family with, share life with, and grow with. With that being said, understand that this person kind of love does exist! However, the most important thing you must know and realize is that THERE IS NO SUCH THING AS A PERFECT RELATIONSHIP. Far too often what people fail to understand is love doesn't have to be perfect; it just needs to be consistent. Therefore, if love is not consistent, it may be concluded that you or the relationship you were once involved in revolved around a "lust-thing" instead of a "love-thing." Real love is consistent; it causes you to endure, it causes you to find a way to make things work with the one you're in love with, and real love causes you to exhaust every avenue possible to overcome any challenge that the two of you may face.

When we talk about this kind of love and relationship, you cannot make this kind of relationship work or this kind of love last when: (1.) you're always looking for a way out if something goes wrong; or (2) you always keep the door of possibility open for those "just in case moments."

To have this kind of love and relationship, you MUST be willing to close all exits without looking for a way of escape. Closing all exits means you're in it for the long haul and that you're fully invested into the success of the relationship with that one person regardless of the challenges and issues that may arise in the future. It is a definitive stance that, regardless of the hurts or disagreements that may occur, you're willing and ready to help each other heal and overcome all discrepancies no matter the extent. In other words, when both parties close all exits no one in the relationship has to worry about who's going to leave or who won't be present later on today because of the issues you may currently have.

"One of the greatest joys is having a spouse with whom you can share your absolute truth without the fear of it being used against you, without fear of being judged or condemned, and without fear of being viewed differently then who you really are."

To be fully committed in a relationship is to be invested so completely in that you have nowhere else to go, nor are you looking for anywhere else to go. It means that you feel obligated to your mate and the relationship and that you will exhaust all possibilities and avenues to guarantee the overall success of the relationship. Closing all exits means that your mate and relationship have your complete and undivided attention. It is a total commitment; regardless of what happens, you're staying and no matter the difficulty or challenge, you're going to make it work. Closing all exits is also an indication that you're willing to become a team partner with your mate, and that you're determined to face this journey called life as a unit instead of as an individual. It means that adversity and hardships won't influence you to run away. Many people shy away from this magnitude of relationship because, with this new age mentality of both the young and old, no one wants to create the life that they desire with the person they desire. They want that life to be already created without effort or sacrifice on their behalf. What are some reasons people don't close all exits when it comes to relationships, commitment, and the people they are involved with?

LOOKING FOR AN ALREADY MADE LIFE

While there is nothing wrong with having expectations and standards, what some call "basic" essentials, necessities, and even the foundation for their relationship is really an expectation of their potential mate being able to afford them a certain life along with a certain lifestyle. So much so that if the person isn't making a certain amount of money, they aren't living in a certain kind of home or can't afford a certain kind of home, or if their potential mate can't immediately improve their life they walk away. Many people, whether they admit it or not, have walked away from perfect relationships or relationships that had all of the right dynamics to become a great relationship because they were looking for "that life" instead of looking for "that person" they could create "that life" with. At this time in society, we encounter people daily who want everything right now and already made. No one wants to build or create the relationship they desire; if they do, they want to build and create from something and someone who's already 90 percent made. People want to come into a relationship doing as little as possible, while at the same time expecting the other person's life and resources to upgrade and improve their life automatically.

This doesn't suggest that you should go find any "Johnny Come Lately" or any "Mary Desperately Anticipating." However, at the moment when you initially meet the person you are to ‘do’ life with, they may not be financially stable; they may not be settled or secure in their career, and their life may not have all of the ideal situations. However, if they show that they have drive, ambition, a willingness to sacrifice and compromise, and they have a plan or vision to improve their life along with doing what it takes for those plans and vision to come into fruition, that's a person you don't pass up on or let go. Yes, that person should be treating you right and loving you the way you need to be loved. However, on the contrary, people would rather go after the person who already earns a six-figure income; who already has the five-bedroom home or can at least immediately put them in one; and whose life is almost problem free. As a result, these same people will be in and out of relationships, or they will have a long tenure being single because they are looking for something and someone who is ready-made.

"Some people won't appreciate you until you're no longer there."

You must be careful with these kinds of people for they never shut the door completely or commit themselves unless they feel that this person has the ready-made life they are looking for. They will date and be involved with whomever until someone comes along who has the ready-made life. It is not that these people can't commit or won't commit, it's just that because of the expectations that they have developed (whether realistic expectations or unrealistic) they are looking for someone who has as close to the already made life that they're looking for. They're looking for a relationship that's based on perks and benefits instead of the person in which they are involved. They don't want to struggle, for their opinion is that they shouldn't have to fight or struggle as much with the person that they're with. They feel that the person that they're with should improve their life or afford them certain pleasures that they cannot afford being single.

HOPES OF REKINDLING SOMETHING FROM THE PAST

Here's an interesting truth that many people know but often don't consider. There are people who have moved on and have begun to date other people because they've grown weary of waiting on their mate to improve or make different decisions. However, though they have started to see other people, there is a part of them that holds on to a hope that their ex would make the change(s) necessary that would allow them to have a great relationship. They get involved with others without fully giving themselves because they still have their hand stretched out to the person of their past still giving them a chance to right their wrong. They wait for the phone call hoping to finally hear from a repentant who may have had unacceptable situations and circumstances, that has now turned their life around. Why, because even though they have started seeing someone else their heart and ultimate desire is to be with the person that they truly love and wish to share life with but felt forced to leave because of their situations or circumstance.

While you cannot control or dictate other people's emotional ties to their past, you can, control whether or not you allow that kind of frustration and drama into your life which will ultimately disturb your peace. You can't, nor should you ever, make life decisions with these types of people. You'll never have balance, you'll never have any stability, and you'll always have to compete for this person's time and attention because they will always be torn between you and the other person or people from their past; it is a breeding ground for a broken heart and disappointment. Often, people who chose to be involved with other people like this are the only ones fully committed to the "situationship," and their commitment is based on wishful thinking. They make decisions regarding this person based on what they could have with this individual if only this individual would let go of the source(s) from their past. The only issue about wishful thinking is, it's not realistic, it’s not promising, and it lacks the potential to have a future. Consequently, if you live a settled life that demands that you commit to someone who's settled as well or at least making progress to be settled, run from that person who proves themselves to still have a hold on people from their past.

"You can't force someone else to fix what other people have messed up in your life."

OPEN LOVE LETTER

Good Morning Beautiful,

Forgive me for being emotional today. However, I need you to know and understand the fear I'm facing this morning; I'm afraid of losing you. I'm afraid of not having you in my life! It's not that I'm insecure or feel as if I couldn't find anyone else; I'm afraid of losing you because I don't want anyone else to take your place. I don't want anyone else touching me. I don't want anyone else kissing me. I don't want anyone else lying next to me. I don't want anyone else holding me. I don't want anyone else living life with me. Nor do I want to make love to anyone else the rest of my life. I don't want anyone else. Our chemistry, our connection, and the compassion we share can't be compared to anything else nor can anyone else be you.

I'm addicted to you. You not only have my heart, but you have my soul. My entire being cries out for you. I'm afraid of losing you because my world doesn't have space for anyone but you. I'm completely and totally invested in you, in us; with all of my mind, my heart, and my entire existence. You have all of me. I've never wanted just one night with you, or just a temporary experience, but I've always seen a lifetime with you. I don't want to lose you not now, not later, not ever...I love you.
Forever and Always,

Your Future

CHAPTER 5

You Don't Make The Rules

Many people wonder why they're still single! They wonder why NONE of their relationships seem to work! They wonder why no one seems to have the patience or tolerance level to deal with them! Yet more often than not, these are the same people who claim that, *their exes wouldn't do right*, *everybody can't deal with them*, or simply *their ex couldn't do what it takes.* The fact of the matter is, many people try to come into a new relationship with a new individual with rules they developed from previous failed relationships. These rules were birthed from disappointment, hurt, secrecy, deception, and even scandal. In other words, because of what they went through with the last person, these rules dictate what has to happen with the next person, or what you're not going to do in your next relationship. This causes the person who has created these rules to continue to live in recycled hurt without allowing themselves to give their all in a new and promising relationship and causes the new person to pay for the mistakes and sins of their former mate.

While you may think that you're protecting yourself and protecting your heart from experiencing that degree of hurt again, you're actually keeping yourself from experiencing real love and companionship. There are a few reasons that your rules are hindering you instead of helping you. Here's why!

"Stop loving people you don't know and stop loving people without learning them!"

YOU DON'T MAKE THE RULES

First of all, you may claim that you are protecting you and your heart until the *right one comes*, here's my question: How do you know when you've met the right one, when YOU are still looking at everyone from a perspective of hurt and disappointment? How do you know when you've met the right one, when you hold everyone's actions or intentions in suspicion due to the ways and actions of people in your past?

Secondly, most of the rules you've made only make sense to you, only apply to the people from your last few failed relationships and were created not even considering your actions in the relationships that didn't work. You weren't absolutely perfect in all that you did and there certainly were many things you could have done better and differently. Wait! There were also some things you shouldn't have done and possibly some things that you may have done in secrecy that just wasn't exposed!

If you've ever been with someone who has either beat you, cheated on you, lived a life that wasn't conducive for you -- and perhaps even your child(ren) if any exist – or otherwise mistreated you, why would you continue to go after a "*Bad Boy*" kind of man?

To all of my brothers, think about the Wild Women you've dated who either couldn't be trusted, damaged your belongings, were disrespectful in front of your child(ren), or just simply weren't wifey material. Why would you continue to seek out that kind of woman?

"People often say that looks aren't everything, however, if truth be told looks is the beginning of a lot of things!"

Contrary to popular opinion, just because a person has a certain status or title, just because a person has money, and just because a person has nice things still doesn't mean that they are right for you. They can have money and be possessive and borderline psychotic. They can have a certain status and title and be completely unstable and unfaithful. They can also have nice things and be just as raged as ever internally and/or mentally. Far too many people are currently in relationships right now and are not even in relationship with the actual person, they are in relationship with what that person has, what they do, what their title is, or with the money they provide for you with.

Secondly, learn to let love develop instead of claiming you're in love three weeks after initially meeting. Yes, I believe in love at first sight! Yes, I believe in an instant connection! Yes, I believe in soul mates! However, be in love but don't be stupid! Don't allow love or your feelings to solely be in charge. Get to know them and don't just be with them just to say that you're in a relationship; study them and learn and get to know them. Stop loving people you don't know and stop loving people without ever learning them! Learn their ways, learn their levels of anger, and find out everything that you don't like about them to see if you can live with your dislikes forever.

Third, understand that everything that's good to you may not be good for you! There are some people whom you should label as OFF LIMITS! It's not that they are already seeing someone else; nor is it the fact that they are common criminals. However, once you've encountered them and found out how their attitude is along with their way of thinking and living, you should know by now to stay as far away from them as possible. Like the character Superman, everyone has their kryptonite. At this point you should know what kinds of people weakens you from a negative perspective. Yet because you've continued to involve yourself with people who have proven to be unhealthy for you, you've gotten the bad end of the deal and have endeavored to create rules that only apply to them, rather than creating rules that will apply to new, and hopefully more positive, person(s) you'll meet in the future. Let's take a moment to discuss why these rules are unacceptable and won't work.

1. Anger

If you were to take a moment to consider the state of your emotions, and even your state of mind at the time you created these stipulations and guidelines, I'd like to call rules. In most cases you were angry, upset, and mad as hell due to the things you had recently found out about your previous relationship and/or the person you were in relationship with. At that moment, you were determined to prevent certain things from ever happening to you again. Honestly, these new rules were your way of trying to make sure that certain things you've previously experienced don't happen to you again. While you should have your standards and expectations, you cannot create rules that only benefit and cater to your needs.

Passion must never guide our decisions when we're angry. When making rules under the influence of these emotions, the rules you make are normally so extreme that they leave no place for compromise or grace. As a result, the rules themselves cause extreme stress and strain on the relationship because the other party, who's trying to live according to your rules is finding it almost impossible to do so successfully.

"Who's with you is not always the one who hurt you!"

2. *Hurt*

The sad indictment is that these rules are preventing you from actually healing from the hurt you've experienced by also keeping you in a position where you relive the same painful feelings over and over again. Yet what is often unnoticed is the fact that rules you create out of hurt sometimes keep you isolated because these rules you've created from this hurt cause you to either push those away who mean you no harm. You may even choose to stay to yourself completely because of your fear of experiencing the same occurrence again, and this causes others to view you as being as unforgiving and unwilling to let go.

Anything created out of hurt never produces compassion or inclusion. It always demands explanation and closure where explanation and closure might not be given. Hurt often demands that someone else pays the price for the behavior of someone who is no longer in the picture. Hurt causes you to hold everything and everyone in suspicion, however, everything and everyone is not the source of your issues(s). You can usually identify the people who've created such rules because they often live under the umbrella of excuses which say, "*I have trust issues*," "*I'll never let another man/woman do that to me again*," or "*I'll never give all of me to another like this in the future.*" As a result, yet another rule has been created and is often used by many who are allowing the hurt to influence their life and decisions. It's a rule that is also used as people's security blanket and is their assurance to not be caught vulnerable. It's a rule that allows them some degree of safety, that if anything goes wrong, they believe that they still have something to fall back on. What rule is this? It's the 50/50 rule. In other words, they give 50 percent and you give 50 percent. When it's all said and done, they say that they want to give you all of themselves, yet they really want you to give all of you while they only give you half of themselves.

If the person you're with is not giving you everything then you should give them NOTHING!!!!!!! Both of you should either be all the way in, or all the way out, PERIOD! Because of the *50/50 notion,* many people will spend their best years, or all of their years, being someone's secret lover, part-time lover, or just a girlfriend or boyfriend due to their fear of going all of the way into the relationship in which they are involved in. What many people fail to acknowledge is, who's with you is not always the one who hurt you. The more critical piece here is the fact that the person who has hurt you has likely moved on three or four times. Yet, you are still holding on to the yesteryears of your hurt and pain, while causing others present-day hurt and turmoil. The disgrace of the hurt that is often ignored is in the fact that the one who's still being influenced by it is often viewed as being bitter and/or vindictive. No one wants to be involved with a person with whom they always have to tread lightly, or with whom they always have to deal delicately, not knowing what will set you off or cause you to relapse and respond out of your hurt.

If I may be permitted to speak bluntly for a moment, deal with your emotional woes and the issues that caused them *before* you involve yourself in another relationship. If you're unwilling to address these issues IMMEDIATELY then you're unworthy of being in relationship with someone who wants to love and be loved by someone freely. Please understand and be very well aware of the fact that no one is obligated to cater to your bitterness or the philosophies that you've developed on your own due to your previous relational dysfunctions. You have to be willing to recognize and appreciate the fact that everyone is not out to hurt, harm, or hinder you. Therefore, you CANNOT deal with everyone as if they are. On more occasions than not, in these instances it is not that they had behavior that was suspicious. However, the insecurities and phobias that you've developed as a result of your hurt have you questioning and second-guessing everything that your mate does. Why? Because you're still allowing the hurt to dominate and control your life and your decision-making.

They've convinced themselves to trust no one and that everyone is the same. Consequently, they've made the decision to allow their past hurts to dictate all of their future decisions. There are just some people you need to LEAVE ALONE, LEAVE THEM WHERE THEY ARE, AND LET THEM BE HAPPY WITH THEIR OWN MISERY!!!! They aren't worth your peace. Nor are they worth you letting someone pass who may be better with less baggage.

3. *Deceit*

While it is true that there are some individuals just because someone from your past betrayed your trust. Every action doesn't warrant you to hold them in suspicion. Every change of behavior is not a sign of sneakiness. We must always be mindful to be in the habit of always treating others (especially our mates) the way we desire for them to treat us. Yet what is often overlooked and misunderstood is that everyone needs their space, their ability to be their own person, and time to do what appeases them as an individual.

"You can't force someone to fix what someone else messed up in your life."

No one wants to be in a dictatorial kind of relationship with a spouse. That is a form of mental and verbal abuse, and in some cases, it can be physically abusive as well. No one wants to come home after a long day to be harassed by their spouse. However, if your only focus in your relationship is to make sure that your mate doesn't get over on you, then you're in a relationship whereby your partner is continuously victimized by your prejudices and insecurities while you expect for them to go beyond the call of duty in order to pacify your selfishness. As a result, people who are mentally and emotionally healthy will run from you. You'll never have lasting relationships, you'll always be emotionally unstable, and you'll always battle your insecurities.

You may say, "*Well, they made me like this.*" While that may be the case, your issue needs to be with whomever "THEY" may be and not take what "THEY" did out on someone new who doesn't even know who "THEY" are. Your mate is not responsible for what "THEY" did to you but you are responsible. You allow what "THEY" have done to have an influence on your future and future relationships.

While no one ever likes being lied to or being lied on for that matter, not everyone is not lying to you, nor do they have something to lie about. Not everyone is conducting themselves with impure motives and there are people who exist who are genuinely attracted to you for all of the right reasons. Many people are still single and will continue to stay single because they possess the mindset that everyone either has something to hide, that everyone has hidden agendas, or everyone has wrong motives. In many instances what, and even how, you think of others is a revelation of what's really wrong with you and what you haven't allowed yourself to heal from. Please understand these important facts:

- LOVE HAS NEVER DONE ANYTHING WRONG TO YOU!
- YOU CAN'T JUDGE ALL BY ONE!

Therefore, you must stop empowering those from your past by inflicting what should have been their punishment on someone who wasn't with you at the time that particular crime against you was committed. No one will cater to your selfishness and insecurities for long, if at all.

Neither *the* failed relationships of your past, nor your gender gives you the authority to make the rules for your next mate or your new relationship. Despite the fact that you may have had horrible experiences in the past, despite the fact that one of your previous mates may have hurt you and may have even taken advantage of you, and despite the fact that it may appear that you're always the one giving and getting the bad end of the deal, you still do not have the authority to make the rules for your next relationship and for your next mate before you even meet them and before the next relationship even begins.

"Being with someone you're not attracted to is an open door to evil possibilities."

However, if truth be told you shouldn't have been involved with them in the first place. You were willing to tolerate certain behavior for insecure reasons, you chose to settle, you were tired of being lonely, or you were simply blind to what everyone else could see. The fact of the matter is, in some instances you played a part in your hurt as well. Yet regardless of the reason behind why you were hurt, how you were hurt, and even who may have hurt you, it does not empower you to have the authority to make rules for a relationship and a mate who had nothing at all to do with the hurt you have experienced in the past. As long as they are realistic and reasonable, you may have certain expectations and certain demands when it comes to how you should expect to be treated. However, you should not make or establish rules for a mate and a relationship that have not yet come into existence. Even once you are privileged to finally meet someone and establish a relationship with that person, you still don't have the authority to make the rules when it comes to the relationship without the inclusion and input of the person you're in relationship with.

1. It's Their Defense Mechanism

Due to the magnitude of hurt they may have experienced previously guarantees that they will never experience that type of hurt again; these rules are their protection, it's the way they cover themselves. These rules help them feel safe. However, when made to feel uncomfortable or threatened, these rules become their safety net and keep them from experiencing a repeat of any kind. Whenever you deal with them, you're really not dealing with them as a person you're dealing with their rules. Their rules keep everyone at bay while creating the illusion of security. As a matter of fact, they have already determined within themselves that no one will ever do harm to them again; when they are really doing more harm to themselves by keeping away someone who means well and could really love them the way that they need to be loved. These rules are their defense mechanism regarding what they actually want and what has happened.

Covering themselves in these rules and allowing themselves to hide behind them gives them a false illusion of security in case anything bad happens that should cause them harm or more hurt. In other words, if by chance they gave you a chance at any kind of relationship, these rules help them to feel secure if anything were to happen that should cause them harm or more hurt. Having these rules tells them that they will be ok if something harmful or hurtful were to happen while they were with you. However, you have to ask the question of whether or not they are really giving you an honest chance at the relationship and in being their mate. For their action and behavior really suggests that they want you to allow them to get close to you and to know you while they aren't affording you the same opportunity. However, if you dare attempt to challenge them on the matter you will get an "*Oh well*" type of answer. The "*Oh well*" seemingly gives you an ultimatum to either accept it for what it is or move on to something or someone else.

Consequently, you really have to ask yourself whether or not you want to be in a one-sided relationship; whether or not you really want to invest your time and frustrate your peace by dealing with someone who has unresolved issues; and whether or not you want to be involved yourself with someone who will never let you get as close to them as you have allowed them to be to you. Are they really worth all of the frustration that comes along with being with them? Are they really worth the time that you would have wasted in which you will

"You can't continually overlook and not acknowledge your mate and expect them to respond accordingly when YOU DECIDE to give them your attention."

never get back? Are they really worth the risk of you missing out on something better to deal with someone who deals with you based on convenience? Hopefully you answer these questions before you develop any feelings and before you stand together at the altar. Your love for a person won't change them! They must be willing to change themselves and take the same risk for you that you are willing to take for them.

2. *To Control the Situation and Outcome*

You will find that people who create these kinds of rules are those who try to manipulate and control the various situations of the relationship, according to their liking. As a result, the entire relationship is only beneficial to them as it caters to their selfishness and self-centeredness. All the while, they are able to hide behind this cloud of rules that dictates you and the relationship but gives them the ability to live comfortably with their own hurt and brokenness.

If you have a conversation with a person who has established rules, or if you question them regarding these rules from this perspective, they will tell you that, "If this kind of situation happens like the last..." or "What happened back then with them will never happen again with anyone else..." or "I'll never be blindsided by another situation or experience like that ever again."

As a result, the rules that they've put in place are to falsely guarantee that they will come out on top if anything was to ever go wrong between the two of you. It somehow gives them the assurance that they will never be hurt again by anyone else in the same manner that their previous mates may have hurt them. These rules, at this point, serve as a buffer against any ill will or fall out with anything or anyone who may have the potential to inflict hurt into their lives. It is their way of keeping you at bay without allowing you to get too close. Yet though they are with you, they really aren't with you nor are they fully committed to you. These rules keep you at a distance while providing them with an immediate way of escape if you ever make them feel uncomfortable or remind them of previous episodes that have absolutely nothing at all to do with you. Being with someone like this, you will never feel or experience true freedom. Them being able to control you and the relationship with these rules keeps everything in a perspective that they "think" the relationship should be. Therefore, if you were to change in any regard, they'd have a major problem and issue with you because you would have moved from the control of how their rules say you should be.

Consequently, this raises a new series of questions that you must ask yourself and provide whom you will never really get to know? Do you want to be in a relationship where you are willing to make all of the compromises while your partner remains settled in their selfishness? Are you ready to handle someone who lives by an open-door policy, coming and going every time something uncomfortable happens? If you cannot answer these questions or you're not willing or ready to be with someone to this magnitude, then you already have your answer to whether or not they are the one or whether or not the relationship is going to work and you really have a decision to make! However, to consent to this type of relationship all because you claim to care for them and to even love them, you are preparing yourself for a possible season, and possibly even a lifetime of misery, chaos, and constant turmoil. Even though you may have moments of fun, the moment you change they will have an issue and you will eventually get tired of catering to them while seeing that they aren't willing to cater to you.

"Knowing your worth is not a justification to be selfish, a spoiled brat, or self-centered."

THE BEST OF BOTH WORLDS
Poem

In case you're wondering how this will evolve or how things would develop with me, I am 'THE BEST OF BOTH WORLDS.' I'm man enough to love you, to care for you, to love you, and to even adore you the way you desire and deserve. I'm man enough to provide for you, to please and to satisfy you, and to protect you the way you've always dreamed of. What separates me from the rest is while others only give you what you ask for or request? I go out of my way and beyond the call of duty to give you what you've fantasized about, to make your dreams a reality, and to make your fairy tales your new norm. What I'm telling you is not game, nor are these mere words of hype just to gain your attention; I'm consistent with it. Why? Because I'm a man of my word. You can trust what I say and expect to see the manifestation of all that I promise because the only thing that would stop me is death itself. Even then, death better come with everything it has because, I'll fight a hell of a fight and try to defeat it before it takes me out. How can I be so sure? With me you get THE BEST OF BOTH WORLDS. I'm hood enough, professional enough, and yet rough enough to bring that seductive excitement into your life that the square ones are not aware of. I'm hood enough to not only give you the confidence but to also let you see that I'm literally down for whatever. There's nothing I won't do, no place I won't' go, no situation I won't confront, and no experience I'll avoid giving you the experience that makes you who you are. I'm hood enough to keep you on edge but secure at all times and in every way possible. I'm hood enough to go from praying with you on one hand to using the vernacular, the verbiage, and words that keeps you feeling professional, rachet, and thuggish all at once without even verbally abusing you whatsoever. I'm hood enough to go from scratching your scalp and rubbing in your hair to pulling you close, oh so seductively and passionately because I know that's how you like it. I'm hood enough to take you from passion to romance to have your most exotic fantasies and wildest fetishes come true. I'm hood enough to be the lover that you always dreamed of. Giving you ecstasy, passion, romance, and intimacy that most people only see on television. I'll make sure we have the soap opera kind of relationship, a lifetime kind of love, to that insane kind of excitement and experience. Yet I'm also hood enough to make you feel obligated to call me your man, you dude, your boo, and your lover all at once. Why, because with me you get "THE BEST OF BOTH WORLDS." I'm spiritual enough to pray for you before you lay down to sleep and before you leave for work. I'm spiritual enough to know when something is wrong with you when you don't say a word. I'm spiritual enough to share with you what The Word says. No need to call the Pastor because I will be your Pastor, meeting the needs of every aspect of your life. I'm spiritual enough to be in-tuned with the inner part of you. Not only knowing what turns you on or gets you aroused but knowing you to the extent that I know your body but your spirit and soul as well. This is why you wouldn't get enough of me. The men you've known were just routine and you were their trophy. However, when you lay with me, know that I've already asked God to show me how to touch beyond your body to actually touch your soul. Thus, our love will consistently evolve. I'm spiritual enough to not only lead you in life but to coach you spiritually into divine destiny and purpose. Other guys only hope God would bless them but with me, because of my spirituality I can tell which direction God would lead us. I wouldn't just simply be your man, your lover, and your friend but I'd also be your pastor, priest, prophet, and king! I told you that I'm spiritual enough. I'm spiritual enough to lay hands on you when you're hurting, to lead you when you're confused, and to prophesy to you when you need direction.

Why, because with me you get "THE BEST OF BOTH WORLDS." Now I'm not sure where you are right now, what you're currently doing, or who you may currently be involved with. Until then, I'm staying in my lane and living in my own world waiting on your arrival. I'm waiting for you to decide that you really want someone like me. However, the day you come and take your rightful place by me you'll then realize that you're not only the luckiest woman in the world but you'll experience a life and romance that you've never known. Therefore, enjoying "THE BEST OF BOTH WORLDS." Patiently waiting...

CHAPTER 6

First-Class Treatment

Due to the fact that I fly quite often, I've had the privilege of flying both Coach and First Class. Yet, what I've noticed is while the flight attendants cater to all passengers, the way the flight attendants handle and treat those who are in First Class is extra personal and attentive. That particular flight attendant pretty much walks through and communicates, caters to, and is involved with those passengers almost the entire flight. This attendant's personality is normally more inviting and extra pleasant. However, what should be more noticeable is while everyone is often served a beverage and snack, those who are in first class are served better, get a better selection of what to drink and eat, and simply get to enjoy the luxury and comfort of flying First Class. While passengers in Coach get to choose from a cart that's rolled down the aisle and drink from a plastic cup. Those in first class have a nicely decorated basket or container of some kind to select from while drinking out of fine glasses, the drinks offered are sometimes different and free of charge.

However, here's the catch: YOU GET WHAT YOU PAY FOR!! While there are those who just paid to have a seat on the flight to get from point A to point B, others paid the price to enjoy the comforts of first-class treatment. These passengers in First Class didn't just want to get from point A to point B, however; they wanted luxury, ambiance, the attention of being catered to, and the feeling of not being treated as average. Here's my only issue with this concept, whether others can afford the first-class flight or not. If someone has paid the price to fly with this particular airline, though they possibly could not afford the price of a first-class ticket or seat if they paid the price shouldn't they be treated just the same? What if everyone got treated on a First-Class level? While some may say you get what you pay for in this aspect, I say you receive treatment according to who you fly with.

After flying on a couple of different airlines, I've concluded within myself that I'm only flying on one particular airline. Why? Because the airline I've chosen to strictly fly on treats you totally and completely different regardless of whether or not you're flying first class. Whereas with the other airlines the presentation is horrible, the atmosphere and environment are uncomfortable, and in some instances the customer service is awful. It's almost as if these particular airlines want you to be grateful that you're flying or that you're on their plane. They don't serve you refreshments nor do they save the seat that you paid for; they call it "an open seat flight.' In other words, even though you paid for the flight and the assigned seat anybody can sit anywhere because everybody on the flight paid to fly in essence. In other words, there are some airlines you need to stay away from and only fly with the airline who treats you the way you want to or need to be treated.

What am I saying here? Perhaps you can't keep a mate, your relationship is on the rocks, or it seems that you season of singleness will never end because you have yet to learn how to give your mate First-Class treatment. I've dealt with couples where one of the two treated other people and strangers better than the one they were in relationship with. To add insult to injury, I've also dealt with couples

"You can't manufacture what a person doesn't have. Either they love you or they don't, they have the capacity to appreciate you or they don't, or they are capable of reciprocating your magnitude of compassion or they can't."

where someone was caught cheating or stepping outside of their relationship, and to the surprise of the faithful mate, the mate that was cheating gave their secret lover better treatment than they gave to their spouse who was waiting at home. They bought the secret lover gifts, went on romantic rendezvous with the secret lover, they role-played with the secret lover, and they even put more effort into satisfying the secret lover than they did their own mate. Let me ask you a few questions according to my opening scenario in this chapter.

What if our attitudes were like the flight attendant in first class? What if we were as attentive to our mates like the flight attendant in first class? What if we catered to our mates like the flight attendant in first class? How can we give our mates this kind of treatment?

1. Create a First-Class Environment

Instead of allowing them to feel that they're just in another relationship with another attractive person, create an ambiance in your relationship that they can't get in any other relationship. Wait, hold on!!!!!!!!!! Before you ask why this is necessary, please understand that there is someone somewhere with a better body and physique than you. There is always someone somewhere who can do many things that you can't do and a whole lot better than you. Also, there is someone somewhere who can show your mate why they are the better person and should be with them instead of you. Thus, EVERYDAY you have to show your mate that you not only appreciate them but why they made the best choice when it comes to being in a relationship with you. Now that we've gotten that out of the way let's continue with this part of the conversation.

FIRST-CLASS TREATMENT

Creating a first-class environment in your relationship encompasses many things. It includes, but is not limited to your appearance, how you talk to them, your attentiveness to them and their needs, you catering to them, the type of relational environment you create for them (how they feel when they are with you), and the things you provide for them. Now let's unpack all of these issues. First and foremost, you ought to take pride in your appearance. It should be one of the things that you take the most pride in; what you look like when you go out into the public eye should be one of the things that you take the most pride in. While your appearance shouldn't be the only thing that you use to attract them, your appearance should be such that it keeps their attention. However, they should not just be attracted to what you look like; you should also give them what they like when it comes to your appearance given the setting, situation, and surroundings.

The thing about your appearance is learning to continually allow them to see in you what they are attracted to. If you notice what they look at, what they comment on, and how they respond to how others dress you can't get offended by it when your appearance is not up to par. You have to give your mate what they are attracted to. We must learn how to present ourselves to our mates and know what it is they are attracted to. It is a compromise we must be willing to make, and it's our obligation! Your appearance shouldn't be the only thing that attracts them or keeps their attention; however, it is a part of giving your mate that first-class treatment.

Your conversation has something to do with creating a first-class environment for you and your mate. Your conversation should be both, comforting, seductive, compassionate, encouraging, affirming, and consoling. You should know how to converse with

"Don't let old hurt ruin new things."

your mate to get the best reaction possible without being condescending or degrading.

2. Give First-Class Treatment

Knowing your worth is not failing to give out the same treatment they wish to receive. How is it that some women claim to be queens and even "wifey material" but when it's time to treat their mates like the king and husband he is, there is a demand for him to do more and be better when they are not doing the same, and vice versa? Or how is it that you demand the benefits of being a queen, a king, royalty, or wifey/husband material yet when it's time to give those same benefits there's always an exception to the rule? In order to shut the door on unwanted guests coming into your relationship and in the life of your mate when it comes to your responsibility, not only must you give them what they cannot find elsewhere. However, you must also treat them in such a way that causes them to overlook everything and everyone else to run back to you.

You cannot expect your mate to always want to run back to a person and an environment that's a disturbance to their peace and their sanity. When you're offering first-class treatment, you're sacrificing and going beyond the call of duty to always make sure that your mate feels secure, they know they have all of you, and they see that you're all into them just as much as they're into you. For first-class treatment to be appreciated, you must be willing to cater to your mate in every way and every area imaginable. However, the issue with this magnitude of treatment is most people fail to cater to their mates because of their insecurities. They cater while somewhat holding back and their justification for doing so is, *that they don't want to appear to look stupid if the relationship doesn't work, or they aren't going to give their all to someone who may not always be there.*

What foolish ideas! If you are afraid that the person you call your mate will do something to ruin the relationship, is being unfaithful to you and the relationship, or may disappear, that says two things. The first thing that suggests is that the person you're with is not the one. Secondly, until you understand that every relationship comes with a certain degree of risks on behalf of both parties, you're not ready for the submissiveness required in a serious relationship. To be honest, that's all submission is! Remember that submission to your mate is not a sign of weakness, nor is it a sign that you're their slave. It's a sign of strength and shows your capacity to love them. You both should be submissive to each other and giving your mate first-class treatment means you not only cater to their needs but you're creative in how you do it and you go beyond meeting their actual needs by touching a higher realm in their lives. Ultimately this causes you to know them at another level to the degree to which you tap into their soul and can anticipate what they may need next.

When you cater to their needs but are also unselfish enough to fulfill their wishes and desires without restraint and restriction, you at that point are giving them first-class treatment. When giving first-class treatment, your primary concern should be to make your mate the object of all of your affections, efforts, thoughts, strengths, and attention. Showing them every day and in every way that they not only have all of you but that they are also getting your best. Whether that be mentally, emotionally, spiritually, or physically. Stop lying to yourself and your mate by saying that they have all of you, all the while knowing that you're holding back and operating with a certain degree of restriction and restraint. You wonder why they may have

"No one wants to be involved with a person where they always have to tread lightly or with who, they always have to deal with delicately. Not knowing what will set you off or cause you to relapse and respond out of unresolved hurt."

wondering eyes and venture off in relationships when you fail to give your all and offer first-class treatment.

3. There Ain't No 50/50 Rule

The mindset of this contemporary culture is, "I give fifty percent and you give fifty percent," expecting a whole relationship while only having half of a relationship. Thus, meaning you have no relationship at all. However, knowing your value allows you to demand all from a person instead of having just some of the person who either has your attention or is trying to gain your attention. Why settle for someone else's less when there's someone somewhere who has no problem giving you their best and all that they have to offer? People who operate with the 50/50 rule are those who are looking for a safety net or a reserve in case the relationship doesn't succeed or last. Consequently, you'll always find yourself giving more and receiving far less. Now don't mistake equal giving for equal sacrifice. Just because a person gives you things and attention doesn't mean that they are giving you all of them.

Knowing when a person is loving you, catering to you, and caring for you to their fullest potential is extremely critical in every relationship. The reason being, when they are giving you their all and their best when you don't recognize it or cannot see it, at that point, you place demands on them that they aren't able to fulfill. Thus, you have to make a decision. A few decisions actually:

1. Considering that this is their best, do they have the capacity to give more?

2. If this is all that they can produce, do you possess the willingness to love them and accept them for the way they are and for who they are?

3. Do they have the potential and capacity to give you more? If they do, are you willing to teach them, coach them, and nurture them to the point to where they need to be?

4. Do they lack the ability to love you and cater to you the way you feel they should, or are your demands entirely too extreme and unrealistic?

In order for your mate to be effective in being with you and giving you all of them, you have to be willing to allow your mate the space to love you and care for you in their own way. Once they've done that, you have to help them fashion who they are, the way they are, and how they are in such a way that compliments you without forcing them to lose themselves. This causes you to learn who your mate is, how they operate, and what makes them tick. When you allow them to love you in their own capacity, that's when you help them learn how to love you to their fullest capacity. However, in loving you to their fullest capacity, they also have to be willing to adjust their abilities to fit and to compliment who you are. Here's why there is no 50/50 rule and why giving your all to your mate is so important. When you have two individuals giving each other they're all, their all compensate for who their mate is not. It's easy to love based on who I am, but the real issue at hand, is your love strong enough and extensive enough to also love me for who I'm not? As a result, when you learn to love me for who I'm not. Your love will help maintain my strength while also causing you to become who I'm not and vice versa.

Consequently, their love for you as their mate says to you that they love you because you're who they aren't. While that same love you give to them, has them loving you for satisfying who they are. Anyone who is not willing to make this type of investment into you as their mate doesn't deserve your space, time, or attention. People who operate by this rule live based on reserve, keeping other things and sometimes other people in place for secondary options. For their mindset is, just in case things don't go right or according to plan they won't be fully invested or left without. All relationships require some degree of risk, and if the person who's supposedly interested in being involved with you is not willing to take that risk, you should be willing to give them a chance.

"When it comes to the relationship, either be all the way in or all the way out."

CHAPTER 7

God and A Garden

I watched a video once of a woman giving her warped perspective of establishing the right foundation for a healthy and effective relationship. Not only was the content of her video disturbing to me, but she also had various social media sites wherein she posted these videos. Subsequently, on that platform, the videos were being liked and shared by thousands as well. As my investigation continued, the more I continued to be exposed to this person, thus, leading me to read the comments posted to one particular video, I noticed how many of her followers echoed and agreed with the tainted philosophies of this individual. Her thoughts seemingly stemmed from an unhealthy place that obviously was cultivated either from the bad relationships of her past or those whom she shared friendship. This proved to be valid and true for the simple fact the majority of the people who commented on the video went on to endorse and consign with what was being said as a result of the failed or toxic relationships of their pasts. Immediately I said to myself and later shared with a friend, that I see why so many people, (men and women) choose to stay single nowadays. The reason being is, far too many people are either spending time consuming unhealthy advice such as this, or they're developing their own ideas regarding relationships based on the many failed relationships of their past. As a result, these ideas they create are found upon safeguards that they've established which are centered around selfishness, self-centeredness, along with many toxic memories of previous relationships you had nothing to do with. Consequently, we now live in an era and culture where the vast majority of people are developing rules, expectations, and demands when it comes to relationships that are extremely unhealthy and unrealistic.

However, there's a greater issue with this sort of mindset and these kinds of people. It is this, anyone who willingly consents to be in a relationship with someone who possesses these kinds of mindsets and concepts endorses them, their behavior, and their mentality as being right when they're completely wrong. I've concluded that people consent to be with people with these warped perspectives for a couple of reasons. Either for sexual pleasure and benefit, thinking they can change them or believing they're just defensive; or merely because they want a relationship to be in to say that they're in one. Whatever the reason for their consent, they are not only supporting this kind of toxic thinking, but they are also causing these types of people to think that they are right due to what they've been through when they're wrong.

Let's get back to the video! The person in the video went on to share how they didn't marry for love and that you should never build a foundation for any relationship that is based on love. The individual went on to say when they met their spouse; they were looking for certain building blocks they felt would benefit them if they were to marry this person and as a result of those building blocks, they learned to love something about their spouse based on the building blocks they were looking for. The building blocks were as follows; what kind of connections did the possible mate have? What kind of resources did the possible mate have? And what kind of network would they have access to in marrying their possible mate?

"If the one that you're with isn't giving you their EVERYTHING, you in return should give them NOTHING."

The person goes on to say that you shouldn't marry for love and even goes as far as to say that Adam and Eve didn't' marry for love, but Adam and Eve married to build... Hmmmmmm! Simply put, what the person suggested in the video is, find someone you can learn to love based on the various things they can offer you in order to give you a better life that you didn't have before you met them.

NOW, let me address a more important issue this person TRIED to address and misinterpreted. Adam and Eve NEVER married to build, NEVER!!!!!! The only TWO reasons God brought Eve to Adam is because Adam was alone and because God wanted Eve to help Adam manage the garden and to be fruitful and to multiply, NOT TO BUILD! When God put Adam and Eve together, all they had was God and a garden. They didn't connect because of building blocks, as a matter of fact, they weren't looking for each other nor did they know each other existed prior to God bringing them to each other. God made Eve for Adam for the sole purpose of keeping him from being ALONE! Once God addressed the alone factor, God then created Eve with the ability to HELP maintain what He had given Adam to do. So, the whole concept of being with someone or basing your relationship on certain building blocks is completely obliterated when you interpret the scriptures correctly. They were brought together for physical purposes! Consequently, to tell someone to get married for any other reason than love and companionship is absolutely wrong and unacceptable.

To marry someone for any other purpose is a clear indication that you're only marrying them for what they can do for you. In other words, you're just using them for your benefit. What's even more sad about this particular commentary is, we've found and created terms to try and justify or even beautify this disrespectful ideology. Terms are used now such as "You need to marry up!" or "I can do bad by myself!" in an attempt to make their behavior justifiable or to sound more acceptable. However, being truthful, we have many people in this day and culture who marry or get involved with people for all sorts of reasons. Some of these reasons may be for business arrangements, to cover certain secrets, to be granted citizenship in certain countries, or to simply improve a life that they themselves have done nothing with. The greater problem with this is people camouflage so well to the degree to which you sometimes can't tell when someone is genuine about you or not. In other words, they only use you for what you have instead of being with you for who you are.

What good does it do to be with someone for the sole purpose of building blocks when there is no compatibility, no physical connection, and no continuity? The fact of the matter is people who marry or get involved on this premise leave when the supposed building blocks crumble or disappear. Many people have parted ways and have even divorced over building blocks either changing or falling apart. Why? Because there was no real love there to keep them together. Love is that component that serves as the glue to any relationship. So much so, that when life changes or situations change, love along with loyalty and faithfulness will make you stay even when issues or situations might suggest that you leave. As a result, the issue and subject matter of relationships should be simple. People on the other hand, have made what should be simple so very complicated because they're looking for building blocks or have constructed their own erroneous rules due to previous failed relationships. So, what happens if a person encompasses the ability to treat you right and to love you right but doesn't have certain building blocks that you are looking for? What happens when a person has the strength and wherewithal to stand with you in spite of your past, in spite of your

---

"Stop making everyone else pay the price for the ones who actually hurt you."

---

flaws, and in spite of your weaknesses but doesn't have certain building blocks that you're looking for? What happens when a person is everything you need and have desired in a mate but lacks the building blocks you're looking for?

Far too many people are single and will remain single all because they're basing everything on what a person can do for them as opposed to what a person can be to them. The fact of the matter is, you shouldn't expect someone to do anything for you that you can't do for yourself. The sad truth is this type of mentality and mindset has infiltrated everything we are involved with. From the music we listen to, to what we watch on television, even in how children are raised; it's all about getting with someone who can do this or that for you instead of being with a person for who they are. The mindset and culture of this day seem to be that of using others, finding someone who will do it for you, and seeing how someone else can make your miserable state better than what it is. With that being said, too many individuals go on a hunt for the perfect person based on these so-called building blocks. When in all truth and actuality, that perfect person doesn't exist. At least not yet! You WILL meet someone who may be, but you will have to help each other to ascertain your "PERFECT SELF" because you're not perfect either!

Here's the problem and issue with being involved with someone based on certain "building blocks." What happens when these supposed "building blocks" erode due to sickness, a loss of job or connections, along with an accident or incident that changes the dynamics of the person's life you got involved with and these "building blocks" being the primary foundation? What happens when that person is no longer in an acquisition of these so-called essentials you felt your mate had to have to help you improve your life? Love has always been the glue that has held any and every relationship together, not certain "building blocks!" To the degree to which, when these essentials dissipate and disappear your love for them will keep you faithful and PRESENT. If you were to ever get to the place of marriage with someone, your vows would specifically say this, "I _____________ take thee ___________ to be my wedded wife/husband, to have and to hold from this day forward, for better or for worse, for richer or for poorer, in sickness and in health, to love and to cherish, till death us do part, according to God's holy ordinance;: and thereto I plight thee/give thee my troth."

NOWHERE in your marital vows would it say to be faithful, to commit, or to be involved with a person based on "building blocks" or until those "building blocks" decay. Loving them shouldn't be predicated on what "building blocks" they may or may not have. Nor should your faithfulness and dedication to them be contingent upon this notion either. To allow your relationship to be based solely on these "building blocks" is very selfish, self-centered, and downright arrogant! Thus, no one should be involved with you because you wouldn't be with them for the right reasons and purpose. What you're looking for is a partnership that's based on contingencies, conditions, and agreements; all of which suggests that as long as they can do this for you or provide that for you, then you'd be willing to consider a relationship with them and learn to love them later! Consequently, many people in today's culture and society come into relationships being both guarded and defensive. They approach people without even disclosing or revealing who they are or what they have because of others wanting to be involved with them based on these "building blocks" or what they have.

Very few people at this point want to be involved with someone based on who they are, nor are they willing to accept someone for who they aren't. It's as if people are looking for other individuals who are already made, already perfect, and already well established. What is often misunderstood and dismissed is the fact that we all come into relationships with some baggage. However, the key question is, does that person have a will, a drive, an ambition, and are they taking the initiative to be better and to have better? No one wants to help or invest in their mate anymore, now the only concern and concentration seem to be the finished product of who or what they think their mate should be. As a result, many are teaching these same warped concepts to their kids. We are teaching our kids, especially our daughters, to whore themselves in some cases to the highest bidder or for a certain kind of person, leaving the average person behind, who may be the best choice for them.

"People who refuse to let go of past relational hurts live under the umbrella of excuses which say, "I have trust issues," "I'll never let another do that to me again," or "I'll never give all of me to another like this in the future."

CHAPTER 8

Fighting Fair

Every relationship will have its share of challenges. Every couple will have their share of disagreements. It is impossible to have two different people, from two different walks of life, with two different pasts, who also have two different attitudes and temperaments and not have any run-ins with each other. You will have some fights! You will get on each other's nerves at times! However, it's how you fight and how you disagree that will be a key element to the success or downfall of your relationship. As ironic as it sounds, there is a way for you to fight fair. When fighting an enemy or a threat, you fight for your own defense and well-being at all cost. Whether that enemy or threat is hurt or even destroyed, you do what you have to do to preserve self. However, when you're fighting with your mate, it should be done in such a way to let them know your frustration and your hurt, but your ultimate goal is to salvage your relationship with them.

There should be a different kind of fight leading to different results as opposed to the type of fight and results you'd have with an enemy or a threat. Your method should be different. Your intent should be different. Your goal and even the reason for the fight should be different. Let me interject this disclaimer at this particular time. I do not support abuse of any kind (physical, verbal, emotional, mental, or spiritual). No one has the right or authority to put their hands on you for any reason! Nor should you subject yourself to that kind of environment or behavior from anyone who does. A man should never put his hands on a woman, and a woman should never put her hands on a man. The reality of every relationship is you will have your share of fights, ups and downs, disagreements, arguments, and even some heated discussions; as some would like to tag them. But knowing how to fight when it comes to your mate is a critical issue to making your relationship work and be a success.

KNOWING WHEN TO FIGHT

Please understand that every fight is not your fight; every argument or disagreement is not yours to win, nor is every issue worth arguing over. As the old saying goes, "Choose your battles wisely." Many relationships and even marriages have been destroyed because someone in the relationship chose to make small matters issues of combat; therefore, they said things and also did things that damaged their mate or relationship beyond the extent that things could not be repaired. Perhaps it was a minor misunderstanding or misinterpret-tation, or maybe you're involved with an argumentative person. Regardless of the scenario, you must learn when to fight, and you must learn that you don't have to fight over everything just because the two of you don't necessarily agree. To take the matter even further, you must also learn how to fight when it's time to fight.

On many occasions when involved in arguments or disagreements, one is yelling because the other is yelling, and one person is angry because the other person is angry. However, the most common that one person retaliates in a certain way because of how the other person approached them about the matter. Nothing but hurt occurs when both people are fighting to prove how right they are by refusing to lay aside personal egos and arrogance. However, I submit to you that there are moments when you should fight, but there are also moments when you should let things go. Why let things go? Because it's not worth losing your relationship, it's not worth destroying your family, it's not worth ruining your reputation with your mate, nor is it worth damaging your mate to the extent that they have problems forgiving you when the situation is said and done.

Far too often, people fight over minor things that one simple conversation or moment of clarification could clear up and rectify. However, when you are dealing with someone who's always defensive, who's all about winning and never compromising, and one who's always ready to retaliate because they feel that everyone is always intentionally trying to do them harm, you will always be in unnecessary fights that don't warrant your attitude or aggression. With some people, it's as if you're always walking on eggshells or dealing with a ticking time bomb waiting to explode. You really can't express your innermost feelings, dislikes, or disagree without a blowup. You really can't share your dislike or disagreement with them maturely without a blowup. Nor can you even attempt to question certain things that concern you without having a blowup. As a result, let's address a few moments when it's time for you to fight.

Please understand that when I use the word fight, I'm not talking about the act of getting physical or abusive to the point of hurting the other physically, mentally, or emotionally. However, when I say fight, I am speaking of aggressively taking a stance to defend you, your relationship, and to correct your mate in such a way where they understand they have done wrong or have wronged you.

"Stop putting patches on BROKEN PIECES Expecting to get a WHOLE PICTURE."

---

1. When your relationship/family has been jeopardized. It's time to fight and to take an aggressive stance when your mate has either done something or has caused something to take place that has jeopardized your relationship or your family. Some examples are when they have had an inappropriate conversation outside of the relationship, when they have abused your loyalty and commitment, when they have exhibited behavior that breached or betrayed your trust, and when they have done anything to deliberately bring an offense to you as an individual.

2. When they have exhibited behavior of irresponsibility as a mature adult. When I speak of irresponsibility in this context, I'm speaking regarding your mate intentionally mishandling money. I'm speaking in reference to them doing things that caused them to put the relationship on the backburner to support their selfishness. Also, those moments where they didn't consider your feelings, your opinions, or your needs as if they weren't involved in a relationship. If truth be told, there are some people you shouldn't even allow yourself to be involved with because they are not responsible at all. They can't be counted on, you can't depend on them, nor can you place any serious expectations upon them because they are not responsible!

3. When there is an attack on your character and reputation. You must defend your name, character, and reputation when it comes to the matter of the public. You must also defend it when it comes to your mate. What your mate thinks of you and how they perceive you is critically important to the health of your relationship. Your character and reputation, when it comes to your mate, can destroy your relationship or it can advance it. If your mate perceives you negatively, it will deter how much they trust you and how they deal with you. You cannot allow your mate to have a warped perception of your character, name, and reputation. When their mind changes about you, your relationship changes with them. For there are many reasons, your mate's perspective can change about you. It could range from what someone has told them about you; it could be a mistake you've made that they may have interpreted the wrong way; it could be due to their misinterpretation of your intentions about a matter. However, whatever the reason for their mental change of your character and reputation you cannot allow that change of thought to become final in their mind.

KNOWING HOW TO FIGHT

Not only is it important to know when to fight, but it is as equally important to understand how to fight. Please understand that there is nothing wrong with a good healthy disagreement or argument. However, you must know how to fight so that your fight doesn’t ruin your relationship, and how to argue with your mate in a way that doesn't destroy your relationship or the person with whom we are involved. We must learn how to be passionate without punishing; we must learn how to be confrontational without being reckless, and we must learn how to be direct without being damaging.

Our words and actions must always be to bring revelation and insight to the problem or issue, but never to breakdown or destroy our mate. The reason being, you cannot wound me and not expect to help me heal. We must stop the cycle of hurt people hurting other people. When we stay cognizant that our mate is our mate and handle them accordingly, we'll cease to disagree and fight with them as our enemy. For if we believe that "our mates" are "our enemies," why are we giving them the position of a mate and granting them access in places within us enterally that only our mates should be afforded?

FIGHTING FAIR

Everything should be different when it comes to your mate. The differences could be how you talk to them, how you treat them, how you look at them, how you interact with them, and even how you disagree and possibly argue with them. You can't argue with me like your enemy and then try to love me as your mate. Nor can you hurt me as if I'm an endangering threat to you and expect me to adhere to you as the love of my life. Your mate should always and at all times receive a different treatment from you during every situation of your relationship. Remember that it is your mate and not your enemy! However, if you feel the need to change their title to enemy, then you're in a relationship with a person that should be dissolved. For there is and should be, a difference between a mate and an enemy!

Consequently, when it comes to your relationship, it's not unusual to disagree nor is it unusual to have an argument here or there. Just because you have a disagreement or an argument doesn't mean that the relationship is over or has to end. Nor does the disagreement or argument need to result in wounding the other person. There must be boundaries put in place that should never be crossed to make sure that the relationship, the connection, and even the love is not damaged between the two of you. Boundaries, no matter how bad or heated the times get between the two of you, will keep you from going overboard or being overly aggressive to the extent that you damage your mate. If you consider your mate to be your mate, treat them as such regardless of your emotions or situation.

"If you not tolerating their disrespect causes them to back up or walk away, LET THEM WALK."

CHAPTER 9

Lovers and Friends or Just Friends with Benefits

Is what you're involved in a real relationship or a *situationship*? Before you develop the mindset and attitude that you're in a relationship and developing feelings and expectations for someone or something that only you may desire, it would behoove you to identify and define what you have and even who you have. Though the two of you may very well have a wonderful connection, the feelings are there, and many good laughs and memories shared between the two of you, it's possible that you are involved in something that's contingent upon the current situation, their personal situation, a convenience, or certain benefits.

Periodically, we select mates because the situation feels good and we enjoy the things that we do when we're with that person. When in actuality, the entire setup could be based on one or both of you enjoying that situation together while trying to run from another situation, that may or may not have fully resolved. One of you could be a rebound for the other, or you could each be coming out of a bad experience, and not wanting or feeling ready for something new or serious; you could be a rebound for one another. Thus, you consider yourselves to make agreements with each other and making rules that the both of you are to abide by with the expectation of enjoying what you share without really crossing the lines of a relationship. However, somewhere along the line, feelings become more intense and emotions that weren't supposed to get involved take precedence, and while you say that you're not in a relationship, in your mind and emotionally you really are. Your communication is regular, you begin to confide in each other, and there are even moments of happiness and laughter. You come to a point to where you still don't consider to be in a relationship, but you're angry if you get the slightest hint that they may be entertaining something or someone else. You are officially in a "SITUATIONSHIP!"

However, the conflicting truth about this subject matter is that a "SITUATIONSHIP" and a "RELATIONSHIP" resemble each other almost identically on every level and in every area. The difference between the two is "INTENTION." This forces the questions to be answered such as: *Is this a serious commitment? Is this a monogamous relationship? Are we expecting marriage and a family? Is this going to evolve into a strong love? Is this really for forever or just for right now? Is there such a thing as cheating between you and I or do we have an understanding of what this is or is not?*

Oftentimes, you can be just simply role-playing without really carrying official titles, while at the same time you can be unofficial and not really have the titles but seriously be committed and involved. As a result, it can be concluded that there's a thin line between a "SITUATIONSHIP" and a "RELATIONSHIP." Thus, causing a relevant question to be addressed which says, *Are you really lovers and friends or just friends with benefits?*

"Stop sending conflicting messages and signals expecting someone to know what you want."

LOVERS AND FRIENDS

So often, especially in today's society and culture, we hear "Let's be friends first," or "Let's establish everything we desire based on friendship." While there's nothing wrong with that and it even sounds good on many occasions. It can sometimes be an ensnarement and even a set-up to be used to a certain degree when you're dealing with someone who knows the right things to say but just wants the benefit of being involved with you, without actually being committed to you. In other words, they may love your company, they may love your conversation, and they may even love that type of companionship. When it comes to that word "commitment," you'll be quickly told that you're rushing things or you're asking for too much too soon. "Keep things simple and just let things happen and evolve," is what you will hear! However, if you dare get too close or attempt to become more personal, you may experience a pushback or a certain degree of distance on their part. While your feelings are developing and growing, you ask them what's the problem or what's going on only to be told that they're not ready, they are scared, they're afraid of being hurt, or they want to slow down.

In case you haven't paid attention, you may not have noticed when it's a benefit to them, and they're happy, but the very moment you attempt to turn up the heat and become more assertive regarding commitment, they push away giving you all manner of excuses and reason. It can be safely concluded that this is just a *'friends with benefits'* type of setup and not necessarily a *'lovers and friends'* kind of relationship.

What happened to the days of our youth when relationships were simple, direct, and to the point with no suspense or guessing? What happened to the times when you learned them as you loved them? What happened to the days where you liked them, learned them, loved them, and laughed with them all at once?

The fact of the matter is, relationships were simple then and lasted longer and I believe that they are and can be just as simple now. However, the issue is we choose to complicate relationships and everything about life at this point. We used to write love letters that were funny, creative, direct, and sweet that required direct answers. Letters that went something like this...

Dear Minnie Mouse,
How are you? I decided to d
r
o
p you a few lines to say that I like you. I think that you are very pretty. I really want to be your boyfriend/girlfriend. Please let me know what you think.

Mickey Mouse
P.S. Do you like me? Check yes or no!
□Yes or □ No

Once we wrote the note, we then took the piece of notebook paper and folded it in that square/rectangular shape; and after we folded it, we wrote stuff on it like, "*For your eyes only*" with real eyes drawn on it. We wrote our initials with signs to let the person know how we felt and our intent (M.M. L/S M.M).

Pardon me for taking a trip down memory lane for a second, but my point is, relationships were simple, funny, direct, creative, and sweet. To the extent that, becoming lovers and friends was a collaborative effort that happened simultaneously. There was no need for complication! You either wanted them, or you didn't, and you expressed what, you meant. There was no stalling or delay! There was no trial period, nor was there testing of the waters! You went all the way in or you placed your attention somewhere else or with someone else. Your decision to be with them wasn't solely based on what they had or didn't have, and it wasn't based on what they could do for you.

Your decision was based on the fact that there was an honest feeling shared between the two of you that compelled the two of you to get closer and more acquainted. This innocent feeling caused both of you not only get to know each other, but you also laughed at each other's goofiness and silly ways which caused you to like each other even more. This behavior caused you to want to be close to them all of the time. It caused you to want their attention so much so that you stayed on the phone minutes and sometimes hours at a time saying nothing but, "What are you doing?" Now don't act like you've never done that before (lol)!

When you're lovers and friends, it means that you get acquainted and allow your feelings to run wild for each other without all of the stipulations, rules, and unrealistic expectations or demands that would be a hindrance if you were still broken and even bitter from things of the past. In the process, you will be enjoying and learning from the moments that happen between the two of you. However, the fact that you are learning them while also loving them and developing love for them allows you to enjoy everything about them without trying to force them to be a certain way because you're set in your ways, therefore, wanting someone to comply with your selfishness and ego. It's simply letting them be themselves while also loving them for who they are as well as who they are not. At this point of innocence, you're helping each other, being there for each other, along with laughing at and with each other. There is complete transparency between the two of you while allowing you to get as close to each other as you can.

Being lovers and friends does not mean that your friendship and relationship is void of conflict and issues. However, you're completely vested into both the friendship, as well as, the relationship. You disagree differently, you argue differently, and you settle differences differently because you know that you will hardly find another friend such as them, nor will you hardly ever share a love with someone else such as you do with them. This type of connection is not based on a situation or convenience, nor is it based on any selfish gain. On the contrary, your need for each other and who you are to each other causes you to fight for each other's success and well-being. Being lovers and friends means that you don't push back or get distance when there's a new level of closeness evolving. It means that you allow the other person in to help conquer all of your fears and insecurities regardless of how uncomfortable it may be. It means that you enjoy all of their company and demand all of their companionship.

"There are those who want to enjoy your convenience but don't want you to have the benefit or pleasure of their commitment and company."

CHAPTER 10

Keeping Score

One of the truths of many unsuccessful relationships is that they can never move forward and truly heal because one or both parties continue to tally up all of the wrongs that the other does. In doing so, they use all of the wrongs their mate does in an attempt to justify their ill will and behavior. Their mate can never really recover from a mistake or folly without being continuously reminded of what they may have done months ago that hurt them. However, to justify keeping score or holding on to the wrong that their mate may have done, the excuse of "I may forgive you, but I won't forget what you did." The frustrating part about your mate keeping score is, you will never hear about it or know what it is until the next argument or disagreement. At that time, you will hear about things that happen months ago along with things you didn't even know you may have done.

If we are to be honest about this type of conduct and behavior, this only intensifies the anger and frustration during your arguments or disagreements. Why? Simply because the mate who you've been keeping score against will feel cornered as you surprise them by bringing up issues that they may not have known or been aware of. All of this leaves them in a position of appearing to be inconsiderate and uncaring because you held them in a guilty light without allowing them to correct what you feel they did wrong. In conjunction with this, they will feel as if you're accusing them of things when they think they have been innocent and sincere since the last disagreement.

Thus, keeping scoring is very dangerous and can be very crippling to a mate who may be trying to do their best to please and satisfy you, only to be made to feel as though there is nothing that they can do to make things or the relationship right. Keeping score is one of the biggest killers to your mate's self-esteem, their confidence, and their enthusiasm to make life with you a good one.

If you've ever been told that you are a nag, or they can't take it when you point out their faults without reminding you of yours; keeping score will always have you reliving old issues that won't seem to go away. These issues will always be a stumbling block to you, your mate, and the relationship when someone refuses to stop adding up the mistakes or faults. However, keeping score comes with the anguish and harsh feelings that existed when the incident or disagreement took place, and this is a clear indication that the healing that is, and was necessary, from the last incident has not yet occurred.

As a result, you have hurt compiled on top of hurt continuing to build that has only been suppressed and not addressed. Therefore, it puts you in a place whereby your relationship is not experiencing the joy and happiness you thought existed. It puts you in an uncomfortable position because you have to walk with precaution not knowing what action will send your mate into another angry tantrum. It's hard to please someone who won't let your past go, but they demand that you don't bring up theirs. There is deceit and treachery of the mate who's keeping score! You spend time with them, you sleep with them, you make love to them, you go to dinner and family functions with them, and you celebrate them on birthdays and other special occasions. All the while they smile, laugh, engage in certain activities and functions; you don't know that the entire time the both of you are sharing these moments, they are watching you closely while keeping up with all of the wrongs that they feel you're doing. You kiss them, but they won't disclose it. You're around them day in and day out, but they won't say anything about it. You're trying to cater to them, but you won't be able to tell that the smallest thing you've done has offended them. However, the very moment you all engage in your next argument or disagreement you will hear about all of the things you've done wrong since the last incident.

You will be surprised, and you will be caught off guard, you'll be left completely clueless in some instances. The entire time you thought the both of you were moving ahead, they have been evaluating everything with a critical eye instead of gleaning and appreciating all of the good that has been taking place. To the degree to which, you've been under the assumption that all has been well, and things were great. They have a different perspective on how everything has taken place because they've been looking for things to add to the list of things that you've done wrong, instead of appreciating all of the things that you've done right. As we share in this conversation, there are a couple of questions that need to be answered. So, let’s address the first question that I'm sure you may be asking right now. Why do people in relationships keep score?

"Don't wait until you see them walking out of the door before you make a decision to try and do right by them."

1. To Wound

As mentioned previously, many people treat their mates as if they were their enemies and when they fight, they do so to inflict hurt and pain! In other words, because of what you have done to them, they want you to see how it feels, and they desire to hurt you like you hurt them. So many times, we encounter people that we have unfortunately fallen in love with who's main reason for counting your faults is to utilize them to cause hurt. It is to punish you as a way of evening the score. However, the difference between the hurt they claim you caused them and the hurt that they're causing you is, the hurt you caused them was unintentional and unknowledgeable but the hurt they're causing you is deliberate with intentionality.

This "get even" mindset is self-destructive to what a healthy relationship could be. For the simple fact, though you should be helping each other to be better, the relationship lacks the ability to be transparent because someone is always on the defense. In fact, pointing out the flaw of your mate is not to demean them, nor should it be done in a demeaning fashion. It is simply to make them aware of the intent of keeping the relationship good. However, there's an issue when your mate is of the mentality that everything you do is intentionally done either out of spite or to deliberately cause them harm. If this is the case and these are your true feelings regarding your mate, WHY EVEN BE TOGETHER? Why even waste each other's time trying to be involved in something that's already tainted and tarnished? The fact of the matter is, when you're constantly doing things and trying to find reasons to hurt me, we're each other's enemy instead of being each other's lover.

KEEPING SCORE

Another reason people in relationships keep score is to destroy the self-esteem or confidence of their mate, especially those who proclaim to be the type of person/mate that they are or want to be. Keeping score in this instance is done to bring ridicule and criticism to their mate's character and to remind them that they aren't all that they profess to be. This is a form of verbal abuse! There's never anything that's said to uplift or to encourage, rather there is always something destructive said to discourage their mate. This form of keeping score is a lethal weapon to your mate's psyche, as well as to their emotional and spiritual state. It is a method utilized to ensure that you can never say anything about them because they're either trying to prove that your words are untrue also, what is often misunderstood is the more they keep score, the more they are ruining their relationship. There will always be chaos, there will always be tension, and there will always be a degree of uncertainty. What's even more unfortunate is that consistently keeping score is often a major discouragement to your mate, leaving them unenthused and lacking the motivation also to put forth an effort to make the relationship work because something will always be pointed out as being wrong by the one who's keeping the score.

"A silent friend is just as bad as a public enemy."

2. To Discredit

On many occasions, keeping score is a tool used to prevent you from trying to correct their errors. You will never be able to give them constructive criticism because they will always try to downplay your observation by bringing to light what they feel is wrong with you and, making what they think you've done is more severe than what you say they've done. In this instance, keeping score is done for the sole purpose of them magnifying your faults so that you can't call out their faults. Many people have issues or struggle when someone tells them where they've gone wrong or errored because they consider that to be negative. Also, there is the proclivity to keep score with the intent of telling you that you're not in the position to talk about them considering what they feel your hang-ups may be.

When you experience the act of keeping score, it's generally at a time when you have unintentionally cornered your mate on an issue that they are unwilling to address, don't know how to address, or were caught by the element of surprise and are too embarrassed to address. However, some keep score because they're just entirely too stubborn to change or are unwilling to make the extra sacrifices to make the relationship work. There are those who can't stomach the truth or reality about themselves, therefore, to keep you from confronting them with those truths they make attempts to discredit what you have to say about them so that they don't have to change. As a result, there's always the need to be in observance of you and your actions with the intent of minimizing your words, thoughts, and opinions about their behavior. This is sometimes done when knowing what you are calling them out on.

This type of behavior exposes a major insecure mentality of your mate along with how they may really feel about you and the relationship. While you would think that if you and the relationship really mean as much to them as they proclaim, they would want to know what kinds of changes and corrections they need to make for the relationship to remain in good standings and to continually compliment you as their mate. Instead, it's always a matter of why you can't say this or that to them because of what you did. Or you're not allowed to try and address this particular issue with me because in their opinion you did that. Or before you try and demand this from me, I feel that you need to make these particular changes about you. A person who keeps score is always trying to find ways to discredit your words and even your approach because it keeps them comfortable, complacent, and even content. However, if you're not careful, you would be convinced to believe that you're always nagging or complaining when indeed you are absolutely correct about your observations.

You CANNOT allow your mate to make you feel insecure regarding what you've observed about them just because they cannot handle constructive criticism. You CANNOT back down from fighting for your mate and your relationship when you notice something is wrong. You CANNOT keep silent while they self-destruct and even exhibit behavior that destroys your relationship and what you have built together. However, as with anyone, it's not always what you say that's the issue. It's how you say what you say and your approach that is the issue most of the time. On the other hand, you will often encounter people who are just defensive from the very onset, regardless of what you say or even how you say it. Consequently, it would behoove each of us not only to find out what a person's interests are, what their goals are, and what they're looking for when it comes to a relationship or a mate. At the same time, we must pay very close attention to how they accept correction,

"While you're looking for a MATCH MADE IN HEAVEN make sure it's real enough to be able to function ON EARTH."

constructive criticism, and even their willingness to make the necessary changes and sacrifices to make the relationship work.

This is normally the battleground where many couples either run into conflict or even come to terms and agreements where the relationship must end. For it exposes people's unwillingness to change while also showing their magnitude of selfishness, self-centeredness, and self-righteousness. Your words, opinions, and thoughts should mean something to your mate. They should matter to your mate, and they should influence and motivate your mate to be a better person for themselves and the relationship. Your opinion of them should matter to them, your concept of their behavior should matter to them, and your offense to any of their actions should be just as important to them as you are showing them any kind gesture.

3. To Justify

When your mate exemplifies behavior of an unwillingness to change or to justify their behavior because they don't want to change, they are showing you and telling you that they no longer have a desire to be compatible with you, which brings us to another reason as to why people keep score in relationships. They want to justify their behavior regardless of how wrong or indifferent it may be. Even if it means that they stand in a position in the kind of relationship and romance they claimed they wanted when you all first met. While there is nothing wrong with being wrong at times, there is something wrong with attempting to justify your wrong because of your unwillingness to change and admit that you are wrong. One way to keep from changing and to defend the wrong you don't want to address is to justify it by highlighting the wrongdoing of your mate and to bring credibility and legitimacy to the wrong they are highlighting in you.

At this point keeping score is done for the sole benefit of the party who's guilty of wrongdoing in the relationship. Perhaps they feel targeted, or their faults are always being brought to the forefront. Whatever the reason, they will often use your errors to justify their behavior and in some cases their words. They'll often say that the reason they acted out was in response to your anger. They'll say that they cheated because either you cheated or they were unsure of what you were doing in their absence. They'll also say that they gave up because it seemed like you weren't interested anymore yourself. They will never take full responsibility or accountability for their actions. In most cases they will never admit that they messed up, they made a mistake, or that they were just wrong. There will always be a justifiable reason for their actions and behavior, and that justifiable reason will always be as a result of what they have accused you of, what they think you've done, or what they feel you've done to them.

OPEN LOVE LETTER

Dear Mystery Woman,

Can I come into your room? Can I come into your space? Can I take a position in your life, can I create memories with you that can't be erased? Can I have my share of you, falling in love, sharing love, and even making love while creating love that's real and true? Can I kiss you where and how I please, making your temper rise as I come on to you? Can I tell you my most exotic fantasies without you making me feel like a fool? Can I tell you my most persuasive thoughts and what I'd like to do with you? Can I be honest about a past I'm not so thrilled about and come clean about my truth? Can I be vulnerable concerning my feelings and not be ashamed to admit that I need you? Can I come in and grab you aggressively without saying one word? Can I be confident you'll never hurt or harm me because you appreciate my worth? Can I touch you anywhere I please without being fearful of you pushing me away? Can I look forward to sharing a world with you where you take me to places I've only imagined? Can I trust you enough to tell you what my fears are? Can I lean on you when I'm down or in trouble without you drifting far? Can I?

Your Forever....

CHAPTER 11

Everyone Has Baggage

The perfect person does not exist!!! There is no such thing as a perfect mate because there is no perfect person. To be honest, there is no such thing as a match made in heaven either. However, what makes some people say they have a match made in heaven or they've found the perfect mate; is the fact they have found someone who has not only accepted them for who they are but who is also willing to do what is necessary to make the relationship work in spite of their flaws and baggage. No matter how much we may not like it, we all come into relationships and friendships with some degree of baggage. Some have more baggage than others. Regardless of how well put together they appear to be, or how attractive they may be, everyone has baggage. Whether they came from a broken home, they have children from an ex, they have unfinished business with old ties, or they have some personal issues, just to mention a few... everyone has some sort of baggage!

Considering the fact that everyone has baggage, you have to decide as to what type of baggage you're willing to deal with. This is critical because depending on what kind and how much baggage they may have can be detrimental to your relationship. A person's baggage can cause tension in your relationship, it can be a strain on your relationship, and it can ultimately ruin your relationship. Everyone is not gifted to deal with your baggage, nor are you gifted to deal with everyone else's baggage. However, the issue is when you stop at what you see on the outside of a person while making the assumption that you're willing to deal with their baggage based on looks. Only to get involved with them finally realizing that though they are beautiful or handsome people, their baggage is just too much for you to deal with.

Regardless of how attractive a person may be, parts of their baggage may be a deal breaker for you. There may be some parts of their baggage that may not be part of their past; however, it remains an active part of their present. Therefore, if it's still an active part of their lives, it means that once the two of you get involved, their active baggage will become a part of your life as well. Now while no relationship has to be complicated, depending on what their baggage is, it can and will complicate the relationship between the two of you. For example, sometimes it's not the fact that they have kids that's the issue. It's the other parent of their kids that's the problem and being with them means that you will have to deal with the issues that come with the other parent(s) of your mate's kids. So, while you're having fun laughing with them, enjoying infatuation, and even envisioning what things could be like based on their presentation, pay very close attention and listen to hear and even see what kind of baggage they are bringing to the table.

On that note, often we sit on the phone or at the table for an evening of dinner in a position of conceit and sometimes arrogance, and we ask the question, "What are you bringing to the table?" We ask this question wanting to know what resources, potential, and even qualities are they bringing to the possible relationship that will not only be beneficial to both of you but to you personally. However, we often fail to be specific and particular when it comes to asking what kind of baggage they are bringing to the table. Don't be shy about asking this question. Don't be embarrassed to ask this question. Don't be ashamed to ask the question. It's your life and your peace of mind you're talking about. Don't be blinded by their looks or even their conversation and promises; you need to know what their baggage is. What are they bringing with them that could be considered as problems by people on the outside? You can do bad by yourself; you already have enough issues personally, and as it is, life is already frustrating enough. You don't need to frustrate your peace of mind any more than what it already is. However, at the same time you can't be so critical of other people's baggage because remember we all have some degree of baggage; and you have baggage yourself.

Consequently, you know that you've found someone worth having when they are willing to accept you and your baggage while also helping you deal with it. This is one of the beauties of any relationship when you are willing to work and help each other deal with the baggage that you each come into the relationship with. You're helping them with theirs, and they're helping you with yours. Which, consequently, provokes growth, both personally and collectively, in the relationship. When both of you have this kind of ethics, you can work through anything, and you can accomplish everything. It also shows that the two of you have no secrets when it comes to each other and that you share total transparency. Let us address some different types of baggage!

PREVIOUS RELATIONSHIPS

Previous relationships can be a very lethal form of baggage, especially if the individual has not completely or properly addressed the situation or the person with whom they were once involved. When there are unresolved issues, such as leading on an ex with empty promises for self-gain and gratification, or when there is an ex who's unwilling to let go and move on, it can cripple and even kill any new and possible relationship. It is so critical to resolving any issues and ties with any previous relationship so that the foundation of the new thing is not affected by anything from the old thing. It is unfair, it is uncalled for, and it is unnecessary. No one should EVER disturb your peace knowing that they still have ongoing experiences with another person or someone else from their past. This is very disturbing especially once you've established a certain degree of connection with a person who has portrayed themselves only to have interest in you.

You typically will encounter this type of experience when you realize that you're dealing with someone who can't stand the person that their ex is with. Regardless of what the reason is, it’s not your issue to deal with. Never put yourself in a position or posture to be juggled by someone who wants to leave where they are, yet they are not willing to let go of everything that's behind them. To continuously entertain such a person will automatically make you insecure and defensive, not knowing when or even if your mate has had any contact or interaction with the person who should remain in their past. In dealing with someone who has previous relationship baggage, you have to understand that you DO NOT have all of their time, energy, or attention. It is a clear indication that you do not have all of their heart, and that your emotional well-being is not their priority. It's not only unfair, but it’s extremely selfish to say the least! This type of behavior will most certainly disturb your peace, your space, and your mental energy.

"Be careful when listening to the bitter exes of others. On many occasions they have negative things to say....
1.) because they refuse to let go and want them back.
2.) they don't want to see them happy with anyone else.
3.) they're too bitter to move on."

EVERYONE HAS BAGGAGE

When you're dealing with someone who has previous relationship baggage, you will find yourself dealing with a person who is in limbo about who they really want to be with. Here's a crazy truth; it is very much possible to care about and be in love with two people at the same time. You can despise and not want to be with one person for who they are or what they do. You can be crazy about this new person in your life and the joy that they may bring into your life. However, because of your magnitude of love and care for both individuals, you can find yourself confused about who you really want to be with. Why? Because of your love and the fact that you are now in love with both parties at the same time.

Consequently, many people find themselves frustrated because they have now gotten themselves involved with the same kind of person. As a result, this kind of behavior brings about confusion and instability and causes you to be unstable. What's even more frustrating is when you allow yourself to fall into the position of trying to convince this person with previous relational baggage that they should be with you, all the while they are battling with these episodes on wanting you today, but tomorrow, they are catering to their love and desire for the person from their past.

While the truth may hurt and even cause you a great magnitude of disappointment, don't also allow yourself to get involved with this type of person. However, the very moment you find yourself involved with and even dealing with this type of person, do yourself a favor and RUN in the opposite direction. There is someone else who's willing, ready, and able to give all of themselves to you as you would give all of you to them. DO NOT put yourself in this kind of position or environment! Save yourself the frustration; save yourself the aggravation; save yourself the irritation. It's not worth it at all! If two people are going to be together in a committed relationship that leads to marriage, both parties need to intentionally make sure that they have COMPLETELY severed all ties and have closed all exits with everything and everyone from their past! To be even more truthful, you should desire to be completely free from anyone from your past to prevent anything from happening to the new relationship which could be everything that you've desired and have looked for.

Another issue with previous relational baggage occurs when you are involved with someone who has a prior relationship. Now, DO NOT misunderstand what's just been said. The children are not baggage; however, the child(ren's) other parent may very well be (no disrespect intended). Especially if the other parent is cantankerous, unwilling to let go, or dispute the fact that the child's parent that you're involved with will have the child around you. While there is absolutely nothing wrong with blended families, as many families there are these days, dealing with a person's ex in this context can be a form of baggage that you're not willing to deal with. However, at the same time, you must also understand that your mate's ex could be reacting and even retaliating because they either don't want to see your mate happy with someone else, or they're bitter over the thought of you enjoying the benefit of what they could have or used to have. Therefore, you must decide whether or not your relationship with your mate is worth having and if you are willing to deal with their ex in order to be with them. If you choose to remain, you also have to make sure that your mate hasn't done anything to warrant their ex to respond to you and your relationship with them negatively as well.

However, before you place all of the blame on them and their ex, "YOU" could very well be baggage to them when it comes to their previous relationship as well. How is that you ask? There are many occasions where two spouses who have children together get along better once they've broken up than they did when they were together. In some cases, they can be close, and may even become closer afterwards than they were during the relationship. This does not suggest that they are still sexually active or that they have a desire to be back in a relationship with each other. However, they recognize that they are better as co-parents and friends, as opposed to, being intimate mates. The issue arises when you're not used to seeing the people who were once intimately involved get along better than they did when they were together; or when you allow yourself to be influenced by others in your circle to believe that the two still are intimately involved because they've never seen it themselves. Thus, "YOU" can become baggage! When you're involved with someone who has children from someone else, and you have to understand that they will still have constant and sometimes close interaction with the other parent of their children.

You also have to understand that unless there is some legal conflict, they will go to the house where their child and other parent live, they will still communicate on a constant basis with the other parent, and in some cases, they may still take family trips together FOR THE SAKE OF THE CHILD. As a result, not everyone can handle these types of dynamics. However, because we live in a society that is so accustomed to cutting people off and becoming enemies with people that you were once involved with and had children with, we typically find ourselves getting involved with people who have issues with you having contact and communication with the other parent of your child.

Consequently, if you find yourself involved with this kind of person, I'd suggest that you don't get involved with them. This is a form of trying to get you to choose between your child and them. That choice should be very easy!!!!!! CHOOSE YOUR CHILD(REN)!!! It is your responsibility as your child's parent to make sure they grow up in a loving, nurturing, and functional environment without having anything or anyone disrupt that dynamic. You should want to be with someone who wants the same thing for your children as well. Sad to say, but there are those who have children themselves who become involved in relationships with people who are not willing to let go of their family to establish their own. There are also cases where the family is so accustomed to being close that they aren't willing to let you and your mate go to establish their own lives and traditions. Then there are cases your mate may refuse to be independent of their family to have a life with you, which causes their family to still have influence and some degree of control of their life.

Let's unpackage this part of the conversation. On occasion, you will encounter someone who has close ties to their parents in particular. While there's nothing wrong with having a close-knit relationship with one's parents, there is a problem when either the parents overstep their boundaries and get involved in the affairs of your relationship. When your mate declines to establish a life of their own outside of their parents' rule, or when your mate puts expectations and demands on you. Everything and everyone should come second when it comes to the relationship that you all have with each other, to the point to that you should be establishing and developing your own rules, your traditions, and expectations for each other. You will never win the war of trying to make your mate choose between you and their parents. NEVER! Especially when their relationship with their parents is close and essentially needed by them.

"Regardless of what someone else may have said or what you may have heard, if they've been genuine and sincere with you they deserve a fair chance."

If anything, you will lose your relationship and your mate trying to make them choose between you and their parents. IT IS NOT GOING TO HAPPEN! Your mate has to be willing to evolve and willing to become their own person while compartmentalizing their various forms of relationships along with the importance of them and the roles that they play. Your mate has to be willing to bring about the establishment with their parents that their relationship with you is private, separate, and independent. Regardless of how much you may want them to do it or try to convince them to do so, it has to be done of their own volition. However, when your mate fails to do so, your needs, your expectations, and even your relationship with them will always come second to the relationship and rule of their parents. If you dare to try to intervene, you will become the issue instead of the issue that you're trying to address. If your mate doesn't see it or understand this particular notion, there's nothing that you can do or say to convince them otherwise — being involved in a committed relationship that is to be successful means that both parties must have their own mind and their own independence. Your relationship won't last, nor will you be able to effectively please your mate when you are continuously controlled and influenced by your family, particularly your parents.

The other issue concerning family ties is when your mate exhibits a certain kind of behavior and mindset due to the type of family that they come from. Whether it be habits, concepts, mannerisms, or certain types of vernacular, all of these can be adopted or even influenced by the type of family that your mate comes from. These are issues that you must look for and investigate before you get seriously involved with anyone. In doing so, what you may realize is that your mate behaves, believes, and has become who they are because of a long history of what's been practiced and passed to them over time due to the type of family they have been raised in. While some things may be corrected and even changed given the right attitude, a willingness to teach, and a certain magnitude of patience, there are some other issues that you may have to decide whether or not you're willing to live with and to accept. Being comical, if you are willing to accept these issues understand that your mate's crazy family now becomes your crazy family!

One major problem with family ties occurs when their family never welcomes or accepts you as being a part of them. Instead of giving you a fair chance to either prove yourself or to show your genuineness, they look for and seek to find every reason why their relative shouldn't be involved with you. You have to understand that in this instance there's nothing that you can do good enough to convince them that you are a good person and the right person for their relative. Consequently, you have to make a decision! You have to decide to deal with your mate and their family if your mate is not an independent thinker. You have to decide whether you're going to stay and fight like hell to prove to their family that you belong, or you have to decide whether or not you're going to ignore their family. You can try to convince your mate to have their own mind while dealing with the challenges of being frustrated by your mate as they go through the emotional changes of trying to be independent. Not saying that your mate or their family can't change, but they may not change immediately, and there's no telling what kind of issues you'll have to experience with them and their family before the change actually takes place.

"You can't blame a person for being insecure when you helped create the insecurities that they have."

PERSONAL SECRETS

Personal secrets can be some very deadly baggage, particularly when there is no transparency or full disclosure. Being involved with someone, seriously involved with someone, will require you to reveal things that no one else may know about you. Regardless of how ugly it may be or how bad it may make you look, you should be able to have full disclosure with your mate and vice versa. Neither you nor your mate should have to find out anything about you from people outside of your relationship. However, often times many relationships become problematic and chaotic because someone in the relationship failed to reveal something about them self and instead kept it a secret. One of the quickest ways to kill any magnitude of trust that your mate has in you is not only showing them that you've been keeping secrets but by also causing them to believe that you're either not telling the truth or that you're hiding something. No matter what the subject is, no matter who was involved, no matter who it was with, and no matter what you may or may not have done, TELL YOUR MATE THE TRUTH!

To those of you who are the ones who want to know, your mate will be more apt to talk to you about certain things as long as you make them secure in telling it and assure them that they won't be judged once they tell it. You also can't use it against them once they unveil what they've held near and dear to their heart. However, to those of you who are possibly keeping secrets, you can't blame your mate for being upset when other people know more about you than they do. With that being said, you shouldn't ever put your mate or your spouse in a position where someone else, (particularly your ex,) can reveal something to them that you should have told them yourself. You'd be surprised at what your mate will go through with you and how they will stand by you through anything if only you would talk to them and show them that you trust them with your truth and with your secrets. However, if you do not trust them enough to reveal what your secrets are, why are you even with them in the first place? More importantly, if you're with someone of whom you do not trust with your secrets that says an awful lot of yourself.

When you're dealing with someone with a certain magnitude of maturity the proclivities you possess that no one is privy to; and the areas where your mate is supposed to represent as the strong one. Secrets also disclose your state of mind, your reasoning, and your motives or intentions. It is knowing you on all levels!

However, keeping secrets and not disclosing them in a relationship can be a killer to what you're trying to establish with your mate. It can be conceived as being deceptive, untrustworthy, and even as a form of manipulation. It is best to be transparent when it comes to your mate so that no one can be catch unaware regarding anything about you, your past, and even your actions. You should want them to know all of you; the good, the bad, and the ugly. It is your way of being truthful and exposing who you are, especially regarding those things and occurrences that could be detrimental to the relationship as a whole.

OPEN LOVE LETTER

Dear Mystery Woman,

I often think of what living life would be like once you arrive and come into existence. I hear you constantly telling me how much you love me, how much you're blessed to have me in your life, along with wanting to live life with me to the fullest. However, if truth be told, I'm the one that's blessed that you ever would be willing to take a chance with me, to risk everything for me, and to afford me with the opportunity to come into your space and your world. I'm truly blessed because of you. My only hope is that I satisfy you enough that I become all that you need, want, and desire. My only hope is that I touch you in such a way that makes you crave more of my feeling and caress. My only hope is that I kiss you in such a way that you become addicted to my taste and pleasure. My only hope is that I not only touch your body but I tap into your soul, filling your spirit, touching your spirit man, and ministering to your soul. My only hope is that as I handle your curves, touching you ever so passionately that your body melts at my every touch. All of which produces warmth and sensation that occurs only because of me. My only hope is that the love you develop for me is the same love you maintain for me. My only hope is to live life with you for eternity.

Forever Yours,

Your Future

CHAPTER 12

You Can't Manufacture Love

The pitfall and entrapment many people find themselves in are trying to create something in someone or in a relationship that does not exist. You cannot help a person create compassion, you cannot help a person create responsibility, you cannot help a person create spontaneity, nor can you help a person create the will to take the initiative. They either have it, or they don't. Another issue that people have is trying to create in their relationship what they may have seen in someone else's relationship. This is a result of, the admiration and respect that they may have for the couple that they have tried to emulate. When in fact, the issue with this notion is the two of you are not them. Just because you've seen a specific behavior or a certain pattern in someone else's relationship, it doesn't mean that the exact same thing will work in your relationship. Another component that people fail to consider is, you and your mate and the couple you may admire are not the same people. You don't have the same temperament, you don't have the same mindset, nor do you have the same needs or expectations.

When you find out who the person is that you're dealing with, and may possibly be getting involved with, you have to make a decision as to whether or not you're willing to deal with someone who may lack certain qualities that you're looking for. You have to make a decision as to whether or not you're willing to settle for someone who doesn't have what you're looking for. You have to make a decision as to whether or not you can live without what you want because of what they naturally lack and don't have. However, if you choose to accept them for who they are not, please understand that this is a form of settling. If you decide to settle understand that you made a choice to settle and there are a couple of things that you have to know.

1. It was your choice to settle for that person, knowing what they lack.
2. They may never evolve into the kind of person that you like or may be attracted to.
3. They may never develop the certain qualities or behaviors that you may be accustomed to or may be attracted to.
4. Finally, in settling you are making the decision to live without certain things that you like, need, or at one point felt were necessary.

Again, deciding to be with someone knowing who they aren't and knowing what they lack is a form of settling. There is no debate about it, no arguing over it, nor is there any more conversation about it. IT IS SETTLING!

With that being said, you are choosing to be with someone in spite of what they don't have means that you have to learn how to create a world and build a relationship with the components that they do already have. It's like building a house. If you're building a 10,000 square foot home, you cannot build a 20,000 square foot home with 10,000 square foot of material. Why? Because you have nothing more to build with. You can only build and establish with the elements and components that you have available to you. People can't give you what they don't have! As a result, it is safe to conclude that you cannot, nor should you ever try to establish, have, or pursue something based on potential alone. You must build with what a person already has. When I speak of building with what a person already has, I'm not talking about money, their connections, or their social affiliations. However, I'm speaking in reference to their ability and capacity to love you, their ability to be affectionate, their drive to goals, their ability to have vision for their life and relationships, their magnitude of maturity and responsibility, their ability to effectively operate under pressure, their level of stability, their level of consistency, their level of competency, and their capacity to help create a life of love and intimacy with you.

Far too often, people get involved with other people thinking that they can help them improve or do better based on the potential that the other person has. Now please don't misunderstand me here. There are some people that we may come across who have the resources and who have the desire, but they either don't know what to do with what they have, or they didn't know they could accomplish certain things with what they have. They are willing, ready, and able to do something with all that they possess if they are with the right person who can help them discover new things to do with what they already have. However, in this context when you encounter someone who may simply be void of certain attributes or potential, you have to make a decision at that point as to whether or not you have the patience, the energy, and even the capacity to deal with such a person who lacks certain things. Please note that you may not EVER find someone who is your absolute equal. Meaning, the both of you are compatible in every area of your lives, yet you may very well come across someone who is more or less advanced in certain areas as you, but there's enough for you to work with and vice versa.

"Why waste time with people who are unsure when there are those who want a definite life with assured purpose when it comes to you!"

Let's get down to business and unpackage this issue. First things first, while scanning through certain social media sites I've noticed many people posting cute little sayings, memes, and hashtags about the face they want someone to love and be into them to the same degree that they are into their spouse. However, I have some questions. You have to see and ask yourself, *Does this person have the capacity to love me the way that I love them? Are they intrigued by you enough and are they attracted to you enough to be into you to the degree to which you are into them?* With that being said, you must make sure that you're not a convenience for them. While also asking yourself do they possess the capacity and ability to give you as much effort as you're giving to them. However, another possibility is that they could very well be giving you everything that they have when it comes to effort and attentiveness. Therefore, you have to make a decision that helps you conclude whether or not their best is good enough for you.

The problem with accepting a person's best is, due to the appetites that we've developed as a consequence of past experiences has caused us to develop certain needs over a period of time. Thus, comparing those needs to a person's ability to fulfill those needs becomes a challenge based on the other person's experience and ability to meet those needs. With this in mind, there's a healthy debate that surfaces which some may deem as fair or unfair. A debate that asks is the person's ability to substantiate or meet your need the issue? Or, has what you been exposed to and experienced, an issue. NOW!!!!! Let's be completely honest with ourselves for a moment. While we all have a past, YES!!!!!!!!! Some of the things that some of us have experienced in our past came as a result of our experimentation with certain things, with certain lifestyles, with certain behavior, and even with a certain type of people. Due to our indulging with these things at certain periods of our lives, we have acquired these tastes and have ultimately developed these needs that certain people we come across and entertain in our present may not be experienced in. Now, another question must be asked and answered; Is what you experienced in your past and at certain points of your past life realistic for the ordinary everyday person to fulfill? Or were those tastes and even needs that you acquired and developed over time created due to you involving yourself in experimentation and fantasy?

When this question is answered, you may very well discover that you could be trying to feed ongoing fetishes that have continued to live in your present that you exploited and played within your past. On the other hand, you may be forced to acknowledge that the person that you're involved with or are entertaining may be somewhat inexperienced or not exposed enough to be with someone like you. Whatever the case may be, they cannot be blamed for not being as experienced as you. At the same time, whether or not they are willing to be exposed to what you have experienced and whether or not they have the capacity and ability to fulfill those experiences is what you have to decide if you're going to remain with them. If we could simplify this part of the discussion the question would be, are your needs and expectations realistic? Or are your needs attached to you indulging in certain fantasies that you experienced in your past?

Another issue that has to be addressed is, does your mate or potential partner have the capacity to love you and to express their love to you? Do they have the capacity and ability to show you what you need to see and to make you feel the way that you need to feel? Everyone wants to feel loved just as everyone wants to know that they are loved by the person that they are involved with. However, it becomes your responsibility to discover how your mate expresses their love for you and towards you. Once you discover how your mate expresses their love and affection towards you and for you, it still remains your responsibility to conclude whether or not how they express their love is sufficient for your need to be shown love. Them expressing their love for you goes hand in hand with their personality, their level of creativity, as well as, their past. Contingent upon these components, how they express their love to you and for you is a result of who they are and where they're coming from. Therefore, if what they're doing and showing is all they know or all they have been exposed to; they may very well be doing the best they can do with what they have because that's all they know.

If what they do is all that they know, they may very well be giving you the best they have to offer. You can't build anything with someone who has shown you their heart and their true interests are not with you. However, many people end up heartbroken and disappointed because they come into relationships with "wishful thinking" instead of seeing things and the person for what and who they are.

"If you have to guess or wonder what their intentions are regarding you, there's a great possibility that may not have clear intentions for you at all."

CHAPTER 13

Is It Worth The Investment?

There are those moments where you may come across someone who's not already made. However, they have enough to work with! They may be making progress towards the individual they are to become. While making progress towards the individual they are to become when it comes to being your mate, and how they treat you as their mate, they are everything that "YOU" desire and want in a mate. They're treating you right, they love you the way that you desire, they're intellectually stimulating according to your expectations, and the feeling you desire from the person that you call your mate is what they give you. However, their only issue as far as you are concerned is there are some things they lack or there are some attributes that you look for in a mate that is missing. At this point, a decision must be made. Do you walk away from this person because of the attributes they may currently lack? Do you entertain the notion of being in a relationship with them because they are everything you want in a mate despite certain attributes that are not completely present at this particular time? Or do you completely ignore them all together and continue to look for the person who you feel is the total package?

Many people are currently single, and some will remain single because of this same issue that we're about to discuss. There will arise moments when you meet certain people, and you have to decide whether or not they are worth the investment. Is it worth you being patient with them? Is it worth you given them a chance at a relationship even though they don't possess certain attributes that you may desire in a mate? Do they give you enough of what you're looking for relationally to work with them and to even wait for them to evolve in other aspects that you would generally look for in a mate? Here's one truth. You can pursue or be pursued by someone who possesses all of the attributes that you're looking for in a mate and not have what you need from them when it comes to a relationship. However, you can pursue or be pursued by someone who may not possess all of the attributes that you're looking for in a mate, but they give you everything that you both desire and need when it comes to a relationship. This forces you to ask yourself and even to re-evaluate what's important, and what's really necessary for you when it comes to the person you are involved with in a relationship.

One of the key issues is that today's individual is looking for a person who is already made, already established in every regard, and is seemingly the total package. It is almost as if they are looking for the perfect person. Please understand that the perfect person DOES NOT EXIST. However, the perfect person for you DOES EXIST! Sometimes that perfect person FOR YOU may need a little help, a little support, and a little work in some cases and it's okay if they're worth the investment. Again, in no way nor at any time should you settle just to be in a relationship, just to say that you're in a relationship, or just to be able to boast or to appear to have a companion to impress the public. At the same time when someone has what's necessary to give you the relationship and companionship that you need and desire perhaps you should consider making the investment. Perhaps at this point, we should address what some of these attributes may be to help you understand the kind of investment you should make and the reason you should make the investment.

"Refrain from allowing people to keep you around to fulfill their selfish ambitions, when they have no intent on giving you a permanent and/or consistent place in their lives."

IS IT WORTH THE INVESTMENT?

Periodically, when it comes to considering a person for companionship, we have expectations for them that we sometimes fail to have for ourselves. For example, we want them to make a certain amount of money, to drive a certain kind of vehicle, to live in a certain type of home, to only have a certain number of children or have no children at all, and to have a certain type of job or career. Technically, some people are looking for these particular attributes because they only want security, the look, and the benefits of being with such a person. While you should have a degree of security and enjoy certain benefits of being with an individual, these components should not be the only reason or the basis you're with them. What happens when, or if, these components are gone?

Having a conversation with someone, they told me of a person they knew who was looking to date someone that was "ALREADY" making a six-figure income. This person they were telling me of was currently disgruntled because they could not find anyone to be involved with who was currently making these six figures. After telling me of the frustrations of this individual, the person I was having this conversation with asked me my thoughts regarding this situation. I responded by saying that they would more than likely remain frustrated and single for a very long time for a few reasons. Either those persons are already married, and their spouses are not letting them go for no reason at all; there aren't a lot of people who make that type of income, or maybe they are just looking at them as one of the crew. I concluded my sentiments by saying this person's problem is that they are so focused on getting someone who's making six figures who may not even treat them right, they are likely overlooking several "NORMAL" income-making individuals who could be everything they need and desire. Because they don't make six figures, this person won't give them a chance; thus, they are still single and frustrated!

Let's continue this conversation about this individual for a moment to convey my point. For the sake of dialogue, we'll call this individual "Blue Butterfly." Blue Butterfly is single and not only single but single AND frustrated that they can't find anyone because they want someone making six figures. Now, Blue Butterfly is not willing to make the investment of being with someone who's not making six figures and bringing on their own frustration because they are passing on so many wonderful people who may be making $40,000, $50,000, $60,000, and maybe even $70,000 a year. Wonderful people who may be intellectually compatible, spiritually compatible, and romantically compatible may give Blue Butterfly all of the attention and companionship desired. Therefore, we can conclude that Blue's match does possibly exist when it comes to Blue's desires for relationship and companionship. However, Blue doesn't see them or entertain them because they don't have a minimum of $100,000 per year income. These individuals Blue is passing on could have the potential to make six figures a year. They could have the ideas and creativity of making six figures a year. They could even have the drive and passion for making six figures a year. The only hold up is that they may need help in doing so, the push to do so, or the support to do so. Though they may not "CURRENTLY" make six figures a year, Blue is missing out on a possibly perfect mate because Blue is unwilling to invest into someone like this for WHATEVER the reason. Thus, leaving Blue single AND frustrated.

"You'll continue to be void of what you NEED chasing after the emptiness of what you WANT."

IS IT WORTH THE INVESTMENT?

When you come across someone who offers you the relationship and companionship you want and desire, the investment is worth being made though they may not have certain attributes that you expect or are looking for. There arise moments when you may have to grow with an individual to the place you desire to be. They may not come in already being or having what you're looking for, attribute wise. If they do perhaps you should consider making the investment. But isn't that settling? No, it's called prioritizing. Many people approach others when they're looking for a mate based on the things they may or may not have, based on the benefits that come along with a person, or how they may or may not be viewed by those in the public eye. They then only hook up with those who may have the attributes they're looking for and end up being with someone or marrying someone just to end up miserable and unhappy. Or they end up being in a relationship or marriage for the looks and security it brings, while secretly carrying-on a second secretive life having an affair with someone who provides them with what they need relationally.

Relationship and companionship are about growing together, evolving together, and building together. While I agree that your potential mate should come into the relationship with something being able to contribute in a healthy way. There are moments where your mate or potential mate will come into the relationship with something that the both of you could at least work with. With this in mind, remember, you may not be able to do some of the things or enjoy some of the benefits RIGHT NOW. You could very well be passing up on an individual that's right for you with whom you could do some things with and enjoy certain benefits with later as you build, evolve, and grow together. Sometimes you get more enjoyment and appreciation from what you help to build as opposed to what was already created. When it comes to our expectations of our potential mates, we sometimes approach them from a perspective of selfishness and self-centeredness. We want them to possess certain attributes, qualities, abilities, and even possessions that we ourselves lack. However, the reasons or justifications that are often given for these expectations and potentials is as a direct result of previous relationships that did not work along with people who caused you conflict.

Certainly, making the investment should be contingent upon several factors. You shouldn't engage with just anyone or make investments into people who are of no benefit to you or your life. NO, this does not contradict the statements mentioned earlier in this particular chapter. Why doesn't it? To have someone who's giving you the relationship and companionship you need and desire, they are putting forth an effort, showing motivation, making the necessary sacrifices to be better and to achieve, contributing at their fullest ability, and are making things happen. These are the kinds of people that you should make investments in, even if they lack some of the attributes that you desire. You DO NOT make investments into people who offer you a good companion, but are lazy, lack motivation, and show no interest in being a better person when it comes to life or their situation. In other words, they may very well be able to give you the feeling you want and may even be able to give you the relationship aspect that you desire.

When we talk about making investments into someone, we're speaking of proceeding with a possible relationship and engaging into companionship with an individual who may lack certain attributes. A person may lack certain attributes where we currently are in life. On the other, there are those who may be in a different place right now in life because life changed on them. For they may very well be the ideal mate for you when it comes to the person they are. Secondly, someone at some point in our lives took a chance with us and gave us opportunities. Why not return the favor? We're so busy looking for things and even people that are already made that we are missing the blessing and opportunity of growing and evolving with someone who's everything that we could ever want and need as a person, as a mate, and as a companion. Don't be so busy trying to buy a finished picture that's someone else's work when you can paint your own, which may possibly be more valuable than the one that's already painted by someone else.

CHAPTER 14

Old School Love

Let's go back for a moment. During the time of the 80s and 90, everything was about falling in love, having a family, making your relationship work, and getting back a love that had been lost. The music we listened to at that time was hinged upon these ideals. The movies and television shows we watched were centered around these ideas as well. Thus, the mindset and culture of people during this time was of this perspective also. People during this time wanted to so desperately to be in love and be in a relationship with that one person they could call their own and, most everyone wanted a family! We had the Cosby Show, and Love and Marriage (one of my favorites). All of which included various iconic TV families that shaped and showed different facets of different families. However, in spite of the different cultures and themes of each show and family, they all were about making relationships and family work and making love last. Growing up, we connected with these families and either wanted to be like them or wanted our family to be like theirs. We were glued to the television set because the TV families addressed the various issues that our families may have been dealing with at that time. In spite of the issues they may have had, they always found a way to make their families and their marriages work and last. As a result, we experienced more relationships working and more marriages lasting.

Perhaps you're not familiar with the tv shows or music of that time. However, if you consider your grandparents, your aunts/uncles and great aunts/uncles, or even your parents for that matter, they had a way to make their relationships work and their marriages last. What's more intriguing is when you get older and reach a certain level of maturity, you find out that their relationship or marriage endured some issues that many people in this day and age wouldn't be able to last one day if they had to deal with just one issue of theirs. You find out the family secrets and dirt, and you come to realize that not only did they make love, marriage, and their relationship last but they also made it work despite some very extreme situations and times. However, when you are finding out some of the things that happened, some of you have been bold enough to ask your elders all that they had been through? In spite of the answers, you may or may not have received the truth. They were fully invested, there were no other options, and family meant everything. While I'm in no way suggesting that cheating, or disrespecting is right or anything to disrespect your spouse or family is right. When the family considered you old enough to know some family secrets, you may have found out that your papa had another family across town or had a few outside kids. You may have found out that at one point your parents actually broke up and lived apart for a season but reconnected and stayed together for thirty years and counting. You may even start remembering the times when your family had fights and brawls amongst each other, but they resolved their issues and made relationship and marriage work. No, abuse is not acceptable nor should you stay in an abusive relationship; however, I'm speaking of bad arguments and major disagreements that ALL families have. In spite of it all, our families stayed together, and people made relationships work.

"You can't ask for my life when you're only willing to give me your hand."

OLD SCHOOL LOVE

Things are extremely different now, EXTREMELY DIFFERENT!!!!!!!! From the music all the way down to the TV shows that have contaminated the mindset of almost every person in this day and age. Nowadays, music is all about sex with no commitment, being with someone while having “side pieces” and multiple affairs at the same time, having back-up plans with other people just in case you and your current "partner don't work, and leaving for any and every reason imaginable regardless of how minor it may be. It appears that hardly anyone appreciates the common bond with just one, its all about how many you can have at one time or boasting of what each one can do for you. The mentality seems to be finding the "ones" who can do the most for you while leaving love on the porch and commitment in the neighboring county. It’s now being bragged on, and people boast about how many different people they can have on each night because they have the ability or the "game" to do it. In this day and age, it is suggested as being a "boss" or "on the come up." As a result, we engage with a culture and generation of people who are excuse-driven when it comes to relationships. Meaning, they look for reasons and justification to leave or to be unfaithful or to go elsewhere with someone else. Now the commitments are contingent upon "ifs" without one party or both parties in the relationship being fully committed.

While I'm all for being contemporary and doing things to remain cutting edge and up-to-date, I am, however, still old school when it comes to a lot of things. In this context, there are some things that couples did "back in the day" that were essential to making relationships and marriages work in today's society. These essentials are practices and perspectives that many people in this culture have completely aborted and annihilated, but they are critical components to building and establishing a strong and healthy foundation along with a healthy relationship. Perhaps there needs to be a return to what had us in a healthy place mentally and physically to make a relationship and marriage work. A return to the music that made us want to fall in love and make relationships work, to television shows and movies that gave us ideas of what family and relationships represented. It's not that this kind of love and relationship doesn't exist anymore; we've just chosen to completely abandon what got us to where we are. Not just regarding the subject matter of dating or relationships, but in every regard. How did people create and enjoy the benefits and disciplines of old school love?

BEING FULLY INVESTED

Being fully invested in relationships in today's society and culture seems to be obsolete. In the current culture it appears that so many people want to be with you, leave the door open, have one foot out of the door, and have another person standing in the yard or at the end of the driveway waiting in case things go wrong between the two of you. There seems to be a divide in many relationships now; here it is your stuff is your stuff and my stuff is mine. However, don't be mistaken; this moment is not a discussion about joining material possessions. When we discuss the subject matter of being fully invested, I'm speaking of being all the way into your relationship mind, body, soul, and might. Relationships of old were centered around the two of them, they were all that they had. Their mates had all of their attention, all of their passion, all of their possessions, and all of their convictions. Their mates were their everything! It was one of the most important goals of those who desire to love, to be in love, and to have a family. The belief about relationships and family in that day was, Family before everything. The mindset of that day was nothing came before family and when all else failed all you had was each other (family).

There was no fear concerning the "What Ifs." On the contrary, the attitude of "old school lovers" (what I'd like to call them) was to do all that they could and needed to do to make sure that they didn't lose their mate. Their focus was on finding ways to make their love last and work instead of looking for ways to get out. They had an understanding that they were all each other had and, in their minds, there was no one else for them other than the one who they were with. There was an understanding that "trials and tribulations" (an old terminology) would come and there was no leaving because of troubles. Thus, this type of mentality caused them to make it past and endure some very critical and difficult times. They made it through poverty, the Great Depression, little to no income, raising ten (10) children at times in a two to three-bedroom home, having employment to not having employment, and having to pull together through some very extreme family issues. Now in my opinion, those days were far more difficult than the times we currently live in. Relationships and marriages are not as strong now as they were then.

No one seems to be fully invested these days, the mentality is completely different and contaminated by all kinds of evil influences. People in this day and age refuse to be fully invested because they're always concerned about having a back- up plan. Now, the mindset of people is "I have to have something to fall back on in case they leave or go crazy." "No one's going to hurt me and leave me with a broken heart, so I'll never give all of me to someone." Or "You don't put all of your eggs into one basket." As a result, everyone only has pieces of whomever they're with. However, the justification for this type of mindset and behavior so many people use for this is that times have

"Wanting you and being willing to do what it Takes to make the relationship work with you is two different things."

changed and people have changed. Being truthful, there are some things that really don't have to change; but because what influences us has changed, we ultimately have changed. Consequently, if you're afraid to fully invest into who you're with, the question that lingers is that really who you should be with? You should never settle or allow yourself to be involved with anyone due to their own insecurities. They are so concerned and consumed with preparing for your departure that they aren't fully appreciating your presence and having you in their life.

To be fully invested means that you're with someone who has all of you and is receiving all that you have to offer. They're your only focus, they are the object of your affections, they are your reason, and they have all of your creativity as you seek to find every way to satisfy and make them happy. You're not trying to figure out when or if they're going to leave or stay because your only focus is to make sure that everything works between the two of you. When you get to this point of investment, you can't just walk away or give up on your relationship, marriage, or even your mate because you put entirely too much into it and them to just walk away or give up. It is a place and posture where your fears, insecurities, and phobias are automatically removed. Therefore, you don't have to worry or wonder if you will lose your mate and relationship just because you may have had a disagreement or life happened. The two of you at this point are totally and fully committed and invested in each other. There is no walking away nor do you give up on each other. In every situation and every moment, you find a way to stay in love and to make it work. Relationships back then were solid while those today are so shallow and built on shaky foundations.

Consequently, the reason why the relationships of this day are so shallow is because we have a society full of shallow people with shallow ways of thinking. There's hardly any substance or steadfastness. Everyone's so sensitive and fearful of the What If's; so much so that many people's expectations for relationships and potential mates are extremely low and shaped by many negative influences.

NO MORE OPTIONS

The mindset of people involved with each other back then was that both of them understood that they had no more options. They understood that they were in the relationship/marriage to make it work and to create a better life "TOGETHER." They some way or another made an agreement that there was no way out, nor was there going to be anything that would come between the two of them to separate them. There was a cohesiveness between the two of them that manifested a bond that is very rare in this day and amongst this generation. There was a kind of companionship they shared that literally caused them to be glued together. Even when there may have been reasons to leave, their minds were made up that they would always be there for each other, no matter what. Through growing pains, faults, and horrible mistakes they stuck together through it all. They found reasons to make love last and to stay together, regardless of how bad things may have been, and the good outweighed all of the bad. At the same time, things weren't maliciously or intentionally done to sabotage what they had.

In this culture people are quick to leave because the mindset is, I can do better, I can find better, and I don't have to put up with it. There is a belief that there is always something or somebody better.

Thus, it’s easy for people to leave and walk away when they feel that it’s relatively easy for you to be replaced. It seems that the commitment is based on a slippery slope of contingencies instead of being in a commitment based on absolutes. The mentality is, I'll be with you if, I'll stay with you if, I'll do this for you if, or I'll love you if. Relationships and marriages in our culture and society will always remain temporary as long as people hold on to and maintain their other options. As a result, you're forced to ask the question of whether or not the relationship that you have is real, especially when it is continually stated that they can live without you, or how much better they can do and be without you, or how there's always someone better who can take your place. There is no sense of oneness or real unity because they are always looking for or waiting for the "other."

It's not a sign of weakness! However, there are other instances and scenarios where the person you are involved with may want you to give all of yourself to them while they only give half of themselves to you. Getting back on the subject, when the both of you understand and come to terms with the fact that there are no more options, an obligation will develop that makes your relationship work. You have to make it work because there's nowhere else for you to go, there's no one else that can take your mate's place, nor is there anything else for you to do but to make it work.

Whoever knew loneliness could be so lethal? The absence of the one you desire causing so much distress...Whoever knew that this kind of love could evolve so quickly? Yet some say that they don't believe in love at first sight...Whoever knew that this kind of connection would go far beyond compatibility? Some people never find this in a lifetime, being so innocent yet so true...Whoever knew that missing someone in such a way would leave you longing just to hear their voice? However, there are those who can go a whole day with no interaction or communication at all; however, seemingly totally unbothered. Whoever knew that something so new could have every indication of being so everlasting? Yet, what's lasted long doesn't always have to be good...Who knew? Who could have ever known?

WHOEVER KNEW

It is often stated and suggested that you shouldn't put all of your eggs into one basket. However, you should. There's nothing that will give your mate the assurance of a secured and promising relationship like knowing that you're completely invested and all the way in. Far too many people are in a constant search of trying to find reasons to either leave or to conquer other options when sometimes the best and only option is the one you already have. To be fully invested and not have any other options means that you pour all of your energy, your creativity, efforts, and passions into your relationship along with the person that you're with. It means to completely engulf yourself into the relationship to the point to where you no longer think of "I," but now your thoughts are hinged upon and centered around "US." Your relationship not only becomes your life, but it becomes your lifestyle, and your consciousness becomes a "US" type of existence; capability anything or anyone in the past returning to rekindle anything from the past. Consequently, it means that your mate is your only option leaving no space or room for anything or anyone else.

CHAPTER 15

When Shallow Ain't Shallow

I've always found it to be interesting how those who either already have who they want, or those who feel a certain way because you won't give them a chance or entertain their proposition, attempt to call you shallow because of the certain things you're looking for when it comes to a potential mate. And to hear their reasoning behind their justifications regarding your feelings or expectations are even more baffling and amusing in some cases. It appears that others would rather you minimize what you want just to have someone or to be able to say that you're involved with a person, just because they either chose to settle or are already happy with the one that they have. However, to try and convince you to comply with their opinions, they attempt to tell you things that may sound good, correct, and even spiritual to help change your perspective. They'll tell you things such as, "*Look at them through the eyes of God*," "*Learn to love them with the love of God*," "*When you get older you'll realize that looks don't matter*," and some would even go as far as to say, "*Having a mate is better than not having one at all.*"

Here are my humorous responses to some of these ignorant and hilarious instructions. *Why do I need to look at them through the eyes of God when I'm the one who needs to determine whether or not I'm attracted to them or not? Why do I need to look at them through the eyes of God when God is not the one who has to say I do to them or live with them in life? Why do I need to look at them through the eyes of God when looks do matter in the physical realm? Why do I just need to accept anybody when I can have the kind of person that I want? Why do I need to love them with the love of God when it's my feelings that will be involved and my feelings that will be hurt if something goes wrong?*

The issue is, far too many people spend the bulk of their time over-complicating life, being overly spiritual, unnecessarily deep, and just simply thoughtless when it comes to life and relationships. There is nothing wrong or shallow with wanting what you want. However, the only problem that may arise with what you want at times is having to wait to get what you want. People will demand that you know what you want only to later try and scrutinize and minimize what you want, or they will go as far as to try and make you feel wrong about what you want. There's nothing wrong with wanting to be with a certain "type" of person. Nor is there anything wrong with having certain expectations or requirements for the person that you desire to be with. However, the only dilemma with your wants, expectations, and requirements is whether or not they are realistic. Yes, in some cases your wants, requirements, and expectations can be completely selfish and self-centered and even derived from a negative past. You're not shallow because you want the person you're involved with to have a certain look, a certain amount of financial stability, or a certain magnitude of intellectual capacity. However, the question that remains is whether or not what you want or requiring is realistic. Truthfully, as mentioned previously, we so often look for people who are somewhat already made or with a certain degree of establishment and success that carry the mentality that we want to build with. And someone who already has a foundation that's already established, when we may very well encounter someone who is meant to be with us although they lack in some, if not all, of these areas. Therefore, causing you to have to establish and build from a foundation that's not fully established or already built.

Being realistic regarding your potential mate does not mean that you have to necessarily minimize your wants or expectations for them. It just means you may have to adjust your perspective to work with where they currently are and what they currently have. In order to build upon that and ultimately arrive where you really want to be relationally, opposed to assuming that you're going to meet or find someone who's already everything that you want and building upon what already exists. You may very well have to help them or help each other evolve to be all you want to be. It's a matter of compromise, sacrifice, and determining whether or not you really want someone enough or care about someone enough to create, grow, and evolve with them, instead of wanting them to already be created. There's nothing shallow or wrong with wanting someone who has a certain body type, who has some magnitude of financial means and stability, who has a certain type of personality, or who has a certain perspective. However, the problem is no one is completely perfect and no one is the total package. With that being said, many people are currently single and will remain single all because they crossed paths with someone who may be the type of person that they're looking for but because they lack in certain areas or don't have everything that you want or are looking for. You passed on them because they were not already made. Many people would rather have what I'd like to call "right now" instead of having a "we can build and get to where we need to be." One requires no work, effort, patience, sacrifice, and compromise. While the other requires work, effort, patience, sacrifice, and a lot of compromises.

WHEN SHALLOW AIN'T SHALLOW

In many cases when it comes to relationships, people try to demand what they don't have and what they aren't willing to give themselves. They either want you to have a certain degree of financial stability when they don't have it. They want you to have a certain degree of flexibility when they aren't willing to be flexible. They want you to maintain a certain body type for them when they aren't willing to do the same for you. Or they want you to forever make certain sacrifices for them that they aren't willing to make for you. You cannot always jump to conclusions or determine who a person is or who they're not based on their current situation and circumstance.

When a person shows and proves that they are willing to do what's necessary to help create and improve life with you, this is a person who you can build with, grow with, accomplish with, and evolve with. They may have the body type or are close to the build you like. They may not currently have all of the money you'd like for them to have. Their current position may be a little flawed and complex. However, the key component is, are they making efforts to improve and be better? Are they putting forth the effort to prove that they're willing to sacrifice for your relationship and a life with you? Are they treating you and loving you according to your liking and expectations? If you answered yes to these questions, my suggestion to you is not to allow this person or opportunity to pass. For the sake of those who want to portray themselves as being overly spiritual and deep, my comment to you is, don't miss your blessing looking and searching for something better! Whether you're looking for something or someone that's already established, or you chose to give someone a chance who's not already established, understand that no matter how polished or unpolished a person is, we all have flaws and shortcomings when it comes to who we are, our lives, and our situations. Again, there's nothing shallow or wrong with wanting someone who has a certain body type, who has financial stability, or who's settled. However, you're only shallow when you're so adamant about someone having everything you want them to have that you pass on someone because they either need improvement in certain areas according to your expectations for a mate. You cannot demand such a magnitude of perfection, especially when you're still working on improving and polishing up your own imperfections.

Let's further discuss why you shouldn't pass on some individuals who may not be the finished product that you desire. Many of you may realize that the person you're looking for may come to you in the form of an individual who's not all the way made up yet. Understanding that while you may have expectations, adjustments to your expectations may be necessary. However, in making those adjustments, you can still have what you want and the type of mate that you want. You may have to put in some work and make some investments to get it. Your dream car may be a Maserati, a Bentley, or a Rolls Royce but you only have the money and financial ability to purchase a Honda Accord, a Toyota Camry, or a Chrysler 300. Now, do you not buy the Honda, the Toyota, or the Chrysler and walk or beg for rides everywhere because you can't buy the Maserati or the Bentley just yet? Now, you buy what you can currently afford while working and making the necessary sacrifices to be able to acquire the vehicle of your choice. With that in mind let's look at what you may be passing up because what you see may not be the ideal pick at the moment.

"Far too many people pass on those who'd love and accept them for their flaws, all to be with someone who wants to have fun with them for a few."

BODY TYPE

Please be clear, and make no mistake about it, no one can tell you what to be attracted to. Your attraction is based on your instinct and your appetency. It's something that you were born with and evolves over time based on your own experiences and tastes. No one can create it in you or place it in you, you just like whatever it is you like. In some cases, it is your acquired taste. There are those who are attracted to slim and petite individuals; while there are those, who like medium-build, athletic, thick, and heavier individuals. Everyone likes what they like, they are attracted to what they are attracted to, and there's nothing wrong with that at all. For many, if not all people you have a limit and a max. If slim and petite is your attraction, you have a max point as to how big you desire your mate to be. If athletic or thick is your attraction, you have a limit as to both how small and how big your mate should be. Yet, if you're attracted to people who are more well-proportioned, you also have a limit as to how small your mate should be.

Simply put, your attraction is your attraction. You're not shallow because you are attracted to what you're attracted to. One of the main reasons there's nothing wrong with what you are attracted to is because when the decision is made, you'll be the one who'll have to see them every day, interact with them every day, and hopefully live with them for the rest of your life. Attraction is necessary because when the makeup is gone, when they're not dressed up, when they have days where they're just plain and simple, and when they're having a bad day personality wise or image wise, you have to still be attracted to them to the point to where you still want to be around them and involved with them.

WHEN SHALLOW AIN'T SHALLOW

Over the years I've seen this issue consistently rear its ugly head. Either someone comes into the relationship trying to change the physical makeup of their mate, or their mate is trying to lose something pertaining to their physique that their partner or mate is attracted to, or someone in the relationship has allowed their physical disposition to get "out of shape" and out of control. Before you attempt to argue that your mate should love you anyway, you are, please understand that this is a selfish argument to make when you already know what your mate is attracted to. When you know and understand what your mate is attracted to you may then realize that how you may or may not look could be the cause of some of the underlying issues in your relationship. Before you argue that you are who you are whether slim, athletically built, or thick, please understand that one of the main reasons your mate is involved with you is because when they first saw you, they were attracted to you. We cannot minimize or disregard the "looks" factor. LOOKS DO MATTER!!!!!! LOOKS DO MATTER!!!!!!! Before a person gets to know you before they find out what qualities you have before they find out where you're from, and before they find out your flaws and habits, one of you initially approached the other "initially" because of their looks and your initial attraction to what you saw.

Before you try to argue that all some people want you for is what they see, my answer is somewhat two-fold. First of all, you are somewhat right in this part of the debate but not in the fashion in which you think. Yes, initially people want you and are attracted to you because of what they see. They didn't know you, they never saw you, or they have been attracted to you but never had the chance to approach or say anything to you. Yes, they initially were attracted to you because of what they saw. However, contingent upon what they initially saw, regardless of who you are, sight is the initial phase of attraction. It's in the nature of creation to go after what you are attracted to based off what you see or have seen regarding an individual. My second response to this particular argument is, if you declare that someone only wants you because of what they see, ask yourself what were you advertising, how were you advertising it, and to what degree did you take your advertisement knowing the kind of attention you would get, or it would bring? This goes for both males and females. Again, LOOKS DO MATTER!!!!!!! There's no way to get around it, nor is there any way to disregard it. You simply go after and approach what you are attracted to once you see whatever you are attracted to. Who's attractive to me may not be attractive to you, and vice versa. The end result is you are attracted to what you see because sight is the beginning of attraction.

Now let's get back to the topic of discussion! It is vitally important that you maintain and keep up the appearance that your mate has been attracted to from the beginning. It's keeping their attention, it's a matter of enticement, and it's a matter of maintaining the interest of your spouse/mate. As much as humanly possible, it is our responsibility to keep ourselves up to par and to continuously offer the presentation that our mates were fond of from the very onset of the relationship. This part of the conversation has nothing to do with self-love, oneness with self, self-respect, or the resisting an outside influence to lose oneself. However, this part of the conversation involves you maintaining the attraction, affection, and appreciation of the person who you're in relationship with. Before you attempt to create yet another argument, let me address what I know just ran across your mind. Having children, health issues, and life changes have a way of affecting your body and appearance in ways that you sometimes cannot control. This is a common-sense issue, and there is nothing that can be done to change that. However, when you intentionally and deliberately do things to alter your physical image in an attempt to follow trends, fashion, or those who appear on television, you must always keep in mind what your mate is attracted to unless you aren't concerned about their interest or maintaining their attraction to you. Before you make the argument that you're doing what you're doing to be healthy, please understand a couple of things. Just because you're slim, fit, or petite doesn't mean that you're healthy; just because you're heavier than others doesn't mean that you're unhealthy; and just because you tone your body, or lose whatever it is you're trying to lose doesn't necessarily mean that you'll look better. Let's be honest; some may say that it's a matter of opinion or that everyone's opinion of you shouldn't matter. We all have said to ourselves in private conversations at some point or another of someone else, "they should have remained the way that they were when it comes to how they used to look." With no disrespect intended whatsoever, I maintain that looks do matter when it comes to relationships and what you or your mate are attracted to.

I recall this particular couple I once counseled. One of the major arguments and issues that tainted their marriage was the wife's weight. In conversating with them, she stated that her husband constantly nagged and harassed her about her weight and losing weight. This made her upset, it made her feel bad about herself, and it made her feel as if she wasn't good enough. Now, before you try to say he was just being concerned about her or he was looking out for her best interest and well-being let me finish the story. When they would get into certain disagreements, he'd bring up her weight. When she caught him emailing another woman and that woman was sending him explicit pictures in her lingerie, he brought up her weight. But here's the issue with his rebuttal and argument, HIS WIFE HAS

BEEN THE SAME SIZE SINCE THEY INITIALLY MET AND BEGAN A FAMILY!!!!!!!!!!

"Don't agitate their space when you know that you're not interested in maintaining their attention."

Initially, he bragged on how attractive she was, how beautiful she was to him, and how he couldn't keep his hands off of her. Now her weight was an issue!!! Get a life (I actually said this to him)!!! She was never small, slim, petite, or athletically built and even when she put forth all of her efforts to lose weight, she was the size that she was. It was who she was created and made to be, period! After she gave him kids, she went back to her same weight. This is why it is so imperative that you go after and be involved with someone who you are attracted to from the very beginning. My response to him later as if he wanted a smaller woman, that's who he should have been with from the beginning instead of trying to make his wife into someone that she's not, never was, and never will be. Go after what you want so you can love what you have.

Another issue that we have when it comes to body type is when you "voluntarily" take it upon yourself to lose or get rid of what your mate is attracted to. You cannot argue or condemn your mate for no longer being attracted to you when you got rid of or altered what they are attracted to about you. Your physical appearance is a major a part of pleasing your mate, it is a part of you physically satisfying them, and it is a part of you keeping them intrigued. While the health fad is running rampant, it is being revealed that you can be whatever size you are and be fit and healthy without necessarily having to change your physical appearance. When we are involved in a relationship, the opinion of our mate is critically important when it comes to the healthiness of the relationship. Although our culture is so adamant about proclaiming self-love, we should first learn to love ourselves the way that we have been created before we try to demand someone else to love changes that we are unsure of ourselves. Why get rid of what got the attention of your mate? Many people lose what their mates are attracted to only to get upset when they see their mate looking elsewhere and at other people who are what they are attracted to. To push the issue even further, there are many women in today's society who have now been influenced by certain television personalities. They try to attain the body of someone they admire in the entertainment world, failing to realize that the person they are trying to become had surgical procedures to "create" the body that they now have. What's also misunderstood is that there are some people who have just been blessed genetically to have the type of body that they have.

In some cases you can stay in the gym all you want and still end up not looking the way you hoped you would. You've done all you could think of from diet plans to workouts and still look the way you were born to look. You end up temporarily changing the way you look only for you to evolve back to the way you were intended to be. Therefore, it's a matter of you being happy with the way you were created in order for you to appreciate your mate being happy with the way you were created.

When you learn to appreciate your own attractiveness and the way you were created to be, you begin to influence the type of people who are attracted to you for you are physically, rather than who people are initially drawn to you relationally based on what they see long before they find out who you are. When you accept their proposal and proposition to be involved, it becomes your responsibility to maintain what you have and what attracted them to you as much as you humanly can. This is not just for one individual, this goes for both parties involved.

One of the ways you can keep your mate from being curious about other things or people and maintain their interest is to maintain and keep up what that are attracted to physically. Keep them coming for more of what initially drew them to you in the first place. Keep them wanting to see more of you, wanting to touch more of you, and wanting to crave more of you physically. Many relationships end in catastrophe because someone either lost or got rid of their sex appeal, their attractiveness, and ultimately the physical interest of their mate.

If you're going to be involved with another individual, one of your primary concerns should be to keep and to maintain their interest and attraction to you, along with fully learning what your mate is attracted to. There is nothing wrong with wanting a better life and being connected to those who can help improve your life and situation. The issue with this notion is when this concept becomes your primary focus or your basis for being with someone; it's selfish and self-centered. For those whose primary reason for being with another individual is initially and solely for what they can do and offer financially, it is a clear indication that you're prostituting yourself and looking for a living arrangement instead of a healthy relationship. What a person can or cannot pay for or afford does not determine who they are. Nor does it determine their ability to love or care for you the way you need to be loved and cared for. It is almost as if in today's society people try to choose mates as if they are a part of a get rich quick scheme.

What's interesting about financial security is that while many people are in search of our concept regarding how much money a person has or their financial security has to be somewhat adjusted. This is not lowering your standards nor is this a form of settling. However, what must be understood is everyone doesn't make six figures. Nor is everyone financially situated in abundance. The flip side to that is, just because you may come across someone who is financially wealthy and secure doesn't mean that they will treat you right or love you the way you need to be loved. People often think that being with someone who has more money means that they will have a better life. While there are also those who choose to live in misery and a sense of unhappiness just to have the money and the life that they think comes with it. This is literally being married to the money and not the individual. This is settling.

While money is needed to live, to function, and to acquire and to establish, it should not be the primary basis on which you determine whether or not you're going to be with someone. There are many cases where people could do better financially if only they had help, encouragement, and exposure. However, while you may say you don't have the time to be someone's motivator, cheerleader, or assistant, that particular mindset is a clear indication that you have a misunderstanding regarding what relationships are all about, what marriage is all about, and what teamwork is all about.

For those who also may say that they don't have time to help build anyone who will love you like you need to be loved, treat you the way you need to be treated, and always honor you as their mate. Would you prefer being with someone who may have money, who may afford you a certain kind of life, but who doesn't offer you the kind of relationship and mate that you need? As long as the person you're with or may be considering being with is giving everything that they have to you and the relationship (financially as well), this is a person that you should seriously consider and give a chance to build and grow with. Yes, finances are important, and financial security and stability are important, but we all must start somewhere. On the contrary, not having a good paying job, not making a certain amount of money a year, or not having a certain amount of money in their pocket or their bank accounts should not be the reason for you not being involved with someone.

Here's what I've discovered over time regarding a few people I've had the privilege of counseling when it came to being with someone who they felt was financially secure. I found that they were people who were somewhat irresponsible and sometimes reckless when it came to their finances. They lacked the ability to budget and manage their own finances, and just because they had a desire to do this and put their desires over their financial obligations. They were people who wanted to continuously splurge regardless of what bills had or had not been paid within their own means and abilities. I'd go as far as to say that people who've learned the harsh lessons of living within their means are responsible, accountable, and live a life that's realistic and sensible. They understand that their financial status won't always be the way it is and they know how to live with what they have until better financial situations arise.

CIRCUMSTANCES AND SITUATIONS

As it has been stated, let's be reminded of an important fact. We all have some form of baggage in our lives. We all have a different magnitude of baggage in our lives. We're all either currently going through something, we've recently gone through something, we're in the process coming out of something, or we still have some residual and lingering effects in our lives from the things we've experienced in our past.

While we all have made statements regarding the status and situations regarding our potential mates, we've placed demands and expectations on them that we don't live up to ourselves, that are unrealistic, and are just plain selfish. We've demanded that they have their lives in order while our life hasn't necessarily been that well organized. However, while everyone should have a sense of structure, discipline, goals, plans, and motivation, no one lives an absolutely perfect life without flaw, discrepancy, or dysfunction; if they do, that is one boring and bland life that will eventually disinterest you.

We all have situations and circumstances that we will need help addressing. Some situations are more severe than others, some are more complex than others, and some are more numerous than others. We all have them in some way, shape, form, or fashion. As a friend once told me, "*You kinda have to pick your poison and deal with it.*" No one is perfect and no one has a perfect situation, yet it's interesting how people try to put so many strict stipulations and expectations on other people's circumstances and situations when they begin to consider a mate.

www.ingramcontent.com/pod-product-compliance
Lightning Source LLC
Chambersburg PA
CBHW070949180726
48291CB00004B/1214

* 9 7 8 1 9 4 2 8 7 1 6 0 6 *